P Burder 15.3.19

A Shaky Start and a Lot of Luck

A Shaky Start & a Lot of Luck

Lindsay Bury

A Personal Memoir

Millichope

Published by Millichope

Shropshire

First published 2018

Copyright © Lindsay Bury 2018

The moral right of the author has been asserted

All rights reserved. Without limiting the rights under copyright reserved above, no part of this publication may be reproduced, stored or introduced into a retrieval system, or transmitted, in any form or by any means (electronic, mechanical, photocopying, recording or otherwise) without the prior written permission of the copyright owner of this book

Printed in England by Anthony Rowe Ltd

To my wife Sarah,

my children and grandchildren

Acknowledgements

This book was written in two hour bursts over a period of nearly three years. I found it difficult to disappear for days at a time to a remote undisturbed location to assist concentration, as apparently is usual for these literary endeavours; day to day distractions and the need to have files at hand made that impossible, but what did make it possible was voice recognition software which enabled me to charge ahead and cover several paragraphs, returning later to edit from the keyboard. I am most grateful for Nigel Hoare for initiating me into the mysteries of this software as well as numerous other tips in using the computer.

I am also very grateful to Peter Burden who has kept a watchful eye on the enterprise from Day One, making helpful suggestions on the sequence of chapters and lay out of the book. In the latter stages he has master-minded the assembly and lay out of the photographs and the final edit of the text. His assistance has been invaluable and central to the completion of the whole enterprise.

Going back a few years, I am indebted to my secretary Linda Collins who committed my life's goings-on to file over a period of over twenty years at the busiest time in my career. Her diligence in doing this made the whole book possible. Our garage in Tugford has been surrounded by a wall of files, often just accounts of board meetings, but I have plodded through most of them and I hope I have got most of the facts right and in the right sequence. One invaluable source has been Peter Pugh's history of ACT and I am grateful for being able to base much of that narrative on this. Annette Gomis has read the book through more than once, making some very helpful comments, and writing a Foreword.

Finally my wife Sarah has read it several times and, with her usual facility, has immediately spotted what was essential in the story and where emphasis should be placed. As a result of her and Annette's intervention, one or two stories have hit the cutting room floor. On reflection I agreed that that was the best place for them.

Notwithstanding the hard work and repeated revisions, which apparently always accompany the later stages of writing a book, I have much enjoyed the whole exercise and hope some of this comes through to the reader.

Lindsay Bury

A Shaky Start and a Lot of Luck

Contents

Foreword by Annette Gomis   3

Chapters

One	Cambridge	7
Two	Childhood and Early Years	19
Three	Millichope and the Family	53
Four	Eton and Teenage Years	69
Five	Horsey Island and My First Job	75
Six	Political Adventure	91
Seven	Marriage and Millichope	99
Eight	Singer & Friedlander	107
Nine	Home Life	119
Ten	Dunbar	127
Eleven	ACT	137
Twelve	Apricot	151
Thirteen	Disaster	159
Fourteen	Life at Millichope – Filling up the Home	165
Fifteen	Sale of ACT – Going Plural	175
Sixteen	The Island of Jura	185
Seventeen	Sharp Technology and Venture Capital	195
Eighteen	Bonanza – South Staffordshire Water	201
Nineteen	Sage and Others	211
Twenty	Wildlife Holidays	227

Twenty-One	FFI, GCP, REGUA and Trinity	235
Twenty-Two	The Millichope Foundation	249
Twenty-Three	The Family	255
Twenty-Four	Music and Friends	265
Twenty-Five	The Future	275

| Epilogue | 291 |

A Shaky Start and a Lot of Luck

Foreword

As Lindsay himself is the first to recognise, this is not a rags to riches story. He was the beneficiary of a privileged education and a considerable inheritance. Yet he and his sister went through what by any standards was a very difficult childhood. He had the good fortune to have received some valuable advice from an enlightened schoolmaster during his adolescence; he told him he would have to make a difficult decision and that it would be impossible to please everyone. This undoubtedly left a lasting impression on him. During his long and extraordinarily varied business career he made shrewd decisions, helped, as he readily acknowledges, by a good dose of luck, and, indeed, several companies with which he was associated proved to be frontrunners in their varied specialities.

This book of memoirs takes the reader through a perceptive and entertaining account of his life and family, the people with whom he has come in touch, the countryside that has been so important to him, his business career and his enduring love of music and commitment to the conservation of nature. His early business career brought him into contact with the worlds of technology and finance, where he was obliged to take big risks to carve out a position. Initially in finance, he worked successively in Schroders, Singer & Friedlander and Dunbar and at the same time he became a founder-investor in ACT, a pioneer in the new computer industry, which made a brief flurry on the world stage. From there he moved to Sage and several other industrial and financial companies, culminating with his chairmanship of the South Staffordshire Water Company, which proved a gold mine for all the shareholders.

A conventional business trajectory perhaps, but as this book reveals, in many respects Lindsay Bury is far from conventional. Just as in business his energy has led him to a number of opportunities, so this eclectic range of interests extends to other fields. Foremost among these, and one which has been a constant in his life, is the matter of the beautiful, historic Millichope, a part of his inheritance, for which he had to find the means to transform into a family home, suitable for living in the last quarter of the 20th century. He and his wife Sarah created a happy environment for their children and a place where their many friends were able to enjoy their hospitality.

There was a brief incursion into politics and a lifelong love of music, a legacy from the father he barely knew. An early enthusiasm for fishing and shooting led, as often happens, to a love of nature and to a desire to try to redress or at least slow down the destruction of the natural life of our planet. Starting at Millichope, over the years he has, with his wife Sarah, worked to improve and restore the natural biodiversity of the estate. Latterly they have done the same on the estate which he acquired on the island of Jura. This interest in the protection of the countryside was broadened in scope to the international arena. Extensive travel all over the world has led to conservation charities and for twenty years he has played a leading role in Fauna and Flora International.

A Shaky Start and a Lot of Luck

Thus, his has been a varied life, through which he has applied himself with enthusiasm and almost boundless energy. These same qualities come through in his description of places and events and of his friends and acquaintances. For those who know him well this account reflects his personality and his unshakeable humour and those who do not know him will discover an acute observer and an engaged participant with a genuinely original and unstuffy approach to life.

Annette Gomis

Chapter One
Cambridge

It is January 2015, and I am standing on top of the roof of Great St Mary's Church in King's Parade Cambridge. It's a freezing cold, but beautifully clear day and the East Anglian sky stretches out to a level horizon for 360°. Farmland is clearly visible beyond the city limits in every direction and one is conscious of the scale of Cambridge, a substantial provincial city, but not yet a great urban metropolis.

In the foreground lies the magnificent suite of buildings which makes Cambridge one of the greatest architectural glories anywhere in the world. Immediately across King's Parade, King's College Chapel is flanked by the Gibbs Building and the Senate House. Further to the east, the Wren Library overlooks Trinity New Court and the eye is led to Trinity Great Court and, at the far end, Trinity Chapel, where my father is commemorated on the role of honour among those Trinity men who fell in the Second World War.

To the right of the Chapel, Trinity Great Gate looms; in my final year as an undergraduate, my rooms were on D Staircase, between Great Gate and the Chapel. Beyond Trinity, St John's Chapel dominates and all around there is the honeycomb of courtyards which makes up the various colleges. Lying beneath my vantage point I see Clare, King's, Trinity Hall, Trinity, St John's and, in the distance across the river, Magdalene. It is a spellbinding view, which brought back so vividly the happy and irresponsible years I spent there over 50 years ago.

Cambridge

I didn't remain on the roof long because the January wind had a real bite and soon I was descending a flight of steep stone stairs. On my way up I had noticed the bell ringing chamber of the tower, followed, many steps later, by a wonderful view of the bells themselves. There is a peal of 12 bells, with a 13th bell to chime the hour; they range from 400lb weight to 2,400lb and were made by Taylors of Loughborough, dating in some cases from the 16th century.

I noticed these details because at the age of 72 I took up bell ringing and, after a long apprenticeship, have achieved a very modest level of proficiency. The notice on the wall proclaimed that the bells are rung by the Society of Cambridge Youths, the third oldest group of bell ringers in the world, and they are rung for services on Sunday and various functions, with a practice session on Monday evenings. One of my most vivid Cambridge memories is of the tremendous sound over King's Parade of the bells of Great St Mary's. Maybe the acoustics of the bells ringing out over King's Parade, with the sound resonating back from the buildings of King's College opposite, made it a particularly good place to hear them.

The reason for this visit to Cambridge in my 75th year was to receive the University's thanks for a modest donation which my charitable trust had been giving them. The University was in the process of building a new £60 million conservation campus in the centre of the city, destined to be called the David Attenborough Building, and this was the subject of the appeal. I had a happy day meeting the director of the project and visiting my old rooms on Trinity Great Court, before further meetings with various dons in biology, botany and other subjects, all forming part of the project. However, the chief pleasure of the day was to recall those years, fifty years ago, when I was an undergraduate, and I spent several nostalgic hours happily wandering around in the winter sunshine.

Looking back, I feel quite ashamed of the way I squandered my three years at Cambridge. Surrounded by unrivalled opportunities in every direction – sport, music, theatre, not to mention academic interests – I seemed to spend most of the time drinking, going to parties, organising parties, talking endlessly, and trying to make up for my woeful inexperience with girls, the result of ten years growing up in all-male boys' schools. I came to Cambridge directly from Eton, where my housemaster, Oliver Van Oss recommended me to go straight to Trinity from Eton at the age of 17, which meant deferring National Service until the end of my period at university. Apparently, Trinity then had an arrangement with Eton whereby they would accept three boys a year purely on the recommendation of the housemaster. This dispensed with the need to take an exam of any sort, and was clearly an opportunity not be missed. So there I was, an undergraduate straight from school, at the age of 17 taking up lodgings in digs, and beginning my university career.

No 28 Malcolm Street, my first Cambridge address, was a depressing little terrace house, although I didn't spend much time there. I was two years younger than the bulk of my contemporaries, who had almost all completed their national service in the Army. In fact, three years later when I had got my degree, I received a letter from the War Office

Cambridge

telling me that my services in the Army were no longer required because national service had come to an end. In many ways, I regret this now and rather envy my friends who did national service, often abroad on rather exotic postings. It also meant that several of my greatest friends in life, the ones I met at Cambridge, were two years older than me.

In September 1957, when I arrived at Cambridge Harold Macmillan was still Prime Minister, over 250,000 houses a year were being built, we were told that we never had it so good and, although the Night of the Long Knives had recently taken place, the Profumo scandal was still to come. Britain was finally crawling out of post-war austerity and the swinging sixties were imminent.

Although I was unaware of it at first, Cambridge saw an influx of extraordinary talent in all areas in the late 50s. In the artistic and satirical arena, my contemporaries numbered Peter Cook, Derek Jacobi, David Frost, John Bird, Jonathan Miller, Christopher Booker, Eleanor Bron, Margaret Drabble and Nick Luard, as well as many future politicians, including Leon Brittan, who became one of my closest friends, and Ken Clarke. My friends from Eton who went to Cambridge, by and large came up two years later after national service. However, I soon accumulated a broad range of friends from a wide catchment area, by no means all of them from public schools. Robert Skepper, Patrick Kearley, Freddy de Louche, David Cobbold, Clive Wilson, Bill Spiegelberg, Humphrey Wakefield and his brother Hady, Richard Storey, John Mansfield and, indeed, many others. All of these, with the exception of Leon

Brittan, who is now dead, I still see regularly.

There was also an entertaining subgroup that we called the ice cream boys; they were mostly Middle Eastern and Italian sons of affluent parents who had plenty of money and threw many of the better parties. For an 18-year-old, fresh out of school, the opportunities to have a good time were quite bewildering.

In a letter of this first year to my godfather, Paul Goudime, I wrote,

> 'My only problems are work and cash and otherwise I live an unclouded existence. I seem to spend every evening either at dances, bridge parties, plays and films or in drinking bouts in people's rooms. The buttery wines are among the best things up here in my opinion and I'm critically working through the châteaux in order to discover the ideal bottle.'

The reference to cash is a reminder of the very large sums we all owed our wine merchants. The time spent at parties inevitably involved a good deal of drinking, and the Cambridge wine merchants had developed to a fine art the extending of credit to undergraduates. I don't imagine they got stuck with too many bad debts but a friend of mine, Allan Massie, who has become a distinguished novelist and columnist for *The Scotsman*, *The Spectator* and other magazines, spent I believe, two and a half years after graduating, paying off his wine bill at Matthews, a popular wine merchant just by Trinity Great Gate. Fifty years later, Alan's son Alex married Lizzie Fletcher, the daughter of my next-door neighbour, Charles Fletcher, on the island of

Cambridge

Jura in Scotland. Alan's family borrowed our house for the party and we enjoyed reminiscing about Matthews's bills.

The spending temptations were all too evident but the undergraduate is also expected to do some work. My subject at Eton in the final year had been history and I decided to continue in the subject at Cambridge. The syllabus was bewilderingly wide. I remember doing tutorials in mediaeval European history with Prof Ullman, and simultaneously England under the Tudors with G.R. Elton, who wrote the definitive textbook on Thomas Cromwell, maybe to be widely used as a source by Hilary Mantel in her bestselling novels. The subject for my finals was Les Philosophes, a group of French philosophical writers.

One interesting friendship from my first year was with an elderly classics don called Andrew Gow. He was made aware of my existence by Paul Goudime, and invited me round to his magnificent rooms in New Court, next to the Wren Library. He was well-known to generations of Etonians as the author of the Gow card, a crib sheet of Latin irregular verbs. He used to invite me round in the evening to drink port and consume Brazil nuts, while admiring his magnificent collection of Degas sculptures. He was probably a repressed homosexual, although this was not evident at the time. At the end of my first year, during the summer term I told him I was going to Italy for my first long vacation, and he gave me a copy of Berenson's *Italian Painters of the Renaissance*, which was very generous of him. 'How I envy you going to Italy for the first time,' he said. 'Be sure to go to Arezzo and look at the frescoes by Piero della Francesca.'

A Shaky Start and a Lot of Luck

I read subsequently that he left the Fitzwilliam Museum 24 works by Degas, six by Rodin, and six by Forain. His collection of Degas, started apparently in 1938 with a black chalk drawing, rapidly increased after the Second World War, when he bought very shrewdly. Gow's lasting legacy at the Museum also lay in the establishment of a fund which bears his name, for the acquisition of French paintings. In 2000, with the support of the National Art collections fund the museum was able to acquire a *'....luminous early landscape by Degas, a purchase entirely in keeping with his own taste for Degas's early work.'*

Imagine therefore my astonishment when, on picking up *The Sunday Times* in 2012, I read the headline: 'Orwell's Eton tutor is named as the Fifth Man, as art critic reveals Andrew Gow was Cambridge Five spymaster. The final member of the infamous Cambridge five spy ring has been unveiled as George Orwell's former tutor at Eton; Cambridge classics don Andrew Gow is alleged to have been the spymaster and confidante of notorious double agent and so-called fourth man Anthony Blunt. The revelation is contained in Outsider 11, the new memoir by Blunt's close friend Brian Sewell who is convinced that Gow was the final piece in the jigsaw. The Cambridge Five included notorious traitors Kim Philby, Donald Maclean and Guy Burgess who persuaded MI5 agent Blunt to join Soviet intelligence.'

Much of my time was spent at parties, and looking out for a girlfriend. There was an overwhelming preponderance of male undergraduates and only two girls' colleges, Girton and Newnham. Most of the girls coming from these establishments seemed to be entirely absorbed in work, with very little time for parties and, indeed, their appearance and, no doubt, the attentions of an 18-year-old were not of great interest. However, there were various finishing schools round Cambridge in one of which my dear sister, Sara, was a pupil. This was called Little Shelford and another one near the station was the Bell School, with a fair number of pretty girls, many of whom were Swedish or Italian. They were mostly the daughters of businessmen and in due course I was to get lucky with one of the Swedish girls.

It's interesting to reflect on how the subject of sex first entered one's life. In my case, I was at a Catholic prep school called Avisford, a small place founded by the then headmaster, Charles Jennings, who was succeeded halfway through my time at the school by his son, Michael. Michael took over from his father and made a number of changes. One day, he summoned all the 12-year-olds to a classroom. We did not know what to expect; it was all a bit of a mystery.

'I expect you have all wondered how babies are born,' he started. I remember thinking I had not given the subject a moment's thought, being far more interested in my prospects in the school rugby and cricket teams. The headmaster then got straight to the point. 'Well, the man sticks his tube up the girl's hole.' He then went on briefly to outline the reproductive consequences of this manoeuvre before saying, 'And that's about it really. Any questions?'

We were all thunderstruck, and filed out of the room in complete silence. One wonders what a modern sex educationalist would have made of it. Michael himself during the war had been very badly burned on the face in a tank. He was a bachelor and he was so disfigured that I remember wondering whether any girl would marry him. However, he did marry a very nice woman and, being a devout Catholic, he clearly practised regularly what he had been telling us because he went on to have 11 children.

Sixty years later, Simon Parker Bowles organised an old Avisfordians reunion lunch at Green's, his restaurant in Mayfair. Michael was the guest of honour and I reminded him about the sex lecture.

'Was it really as bad as that?' he asked.

'I'm afraid it was, Michael,' I replied, and we laughed a lot.

A month later, I went to have tea with him and his wife at their home in Hereford. He died very shortly afterwards.

Anyhow, during my time at Eton, sex consisted mainly of adolescent fumblings in the holidays with friends' sisters until, during my final summer after leaving Eton, I went to Paris where Paul Goudime had arranged for me to stay with a family. It was a large family and they lived in a substantial flat on the Chaussée de la Muette in the fashionable 16eme *arrondissement.* Several generations of the family seemed to live there, and the matriarch was a huge, fleshy woman called Madame Eduard Pratt, who'd been an opera singer. She would install herself at the head of the table at meal times, well in advance of everybody else, and tuck in.

On one occasion, when rabbit was on the menu, she sucked extensively at the carcass before detaching the head, which she passed to me. 'Tiens Lindsay,' she commanded.

Cambridge

'Mange la tête!'

I did as I was told.

There was a piano in the living room upon which I sometimes practised scales and other exercises. Madam Pratt, who was a proper musician, was rightly dismissive. 'Lindsay, tu ne sais pas comment faire les exercices.'

She was right, of course. Not knowing how to practise has held me back all my life.

To improve my French, I attended a course at the Alliance Francaise, which involved taking the Metro across the left bank of the city and I still remember the exotic names of the stations, Segur, Duroc, Vaneau, and I would get out at Sevres-Babylone. Leisure hours were spent with two other old Etonians, Charlie Hornby and Jonathan Cecil, son of Lord David Cecil, the historian. Sent there to learn French, we were all in the same position; surrounded by pretty girls in Paris and a complete absence of opportunities to get to know any of them.

Luckily, I did in due course meet an attractive Italian at the Alliance Francaise; Monica was dark haired and pretty, and came from Perugia. We would go to a café in St Germain and talk interminably about the world, religion and, indeed, everything under the sun (in English I am ashamed to say). However I didn't dare to invite her back to the flat which was dominated by the formidable Madame Eduard Pratt and so the relationship didn't progress very far.

So, fast forward to Cambridge and, as can be imagined, girls were a major preoccupation for all of us. Before long I had met Anita, one of a pair of Swedish twins at the Bell School in Cambridge. They were both blonde and attractive;

A Shaky Start and a Lot of Luck

Anita was less conventionally pretty than her sister but was altogether more sexy with an alluring voice and a habit of narrowing her eyes when saying something flirtatious, which I found irresistible. For most of my last two years, we spent a lot of time together. She would accompany me on weekends to Shropshire and Horsey Island, and invited me to stay with her family in Norkoping, about fifty miles south of Stockholm. She was experienced with men, having had a number of older boyfriends, and thanks to her, I finally grew up a bit. Like many twins she and her sister Christina were inseparable and it was lucky that David Cobbold, one of my close friends from Eton, fancied Christina (among many, many others!). After leaving university, the girls went on to marry two best friends and lived in Geneva for the rest of their lives, spending, I later heard, most of every day in each other's houses.

Cambridge, particularly in the summer, was a wonderfully romantic place. The backs, which lead down from the colleges to the River Cam, had beautiful gardens and the river itself was overhung with willow trees, under which we would punt along with our girlfriends and picnic in nice places. It was easy to lose all sense of time; there was no necessity to go to any lectures. Inevitably, the lecturer had written a book; one could just as well read that without going to hear him as well. In the evenings the colleges were locked after a certain hour, but we became quite adept at climbing over the walls and gaining access by whatever means. By my third year not much had changed, except our choice of friends had settled down and we became increasingly conscious that exams were pending, and there was an uneasy sense that we had work to do. Finally, I did manage to get a 2.1 in the history Tripos, which was a great relief, and a considerable surprise to my tutor who had taken a dim view of the effort I was putting in.

Reading all this through in later years, it does seem to have been a shameful waste of time, which could have been more profitably spent in organised sports or taking advantage of the innumerable facilities which Cambridge had to offer. This was not to be, but at least I did finish up with a reasonable degree and a group of friends who have remained close all my life.

Chapter Two
Childhood and Early Years

Both my parents died young, at the age of 33. My father, Frank Bury was born in 1911 and was killed in Normandy on 11 July 1944, just over a month after the first D-Day landings. My mother, Diana, was born in 1914 and died during the birth of her third child in 1947. Thus, my younger and only sister Sara and I were orphaned, at the ages of eight and six.

My father had grown up at Millichope and had been educated at Eton and Trinity College Cambridge, where he read music. He had always had a great love and obvious talent for music and, on leaving university in 1932, he wanted to make a career as a musician. Following a year at the Royal College of Music in London, he became a conductor and composer. It is a cause of great sadness to me that I can barely remember my father. I have a memory of him holding me upside down when I was about four years old, on one of his rare visits home on leave from the Army. Apart from that, there's nothing.

Up until the war, he worked as a musician and I am proud to possess one of his compositions - a prelude and fugue for two pianos. It is an excellent composition which I came across among his papers. I showed it to a friend and professional concert pianist, Anthony Goldstone, who edited it, had it published and made a recording, as well as performing the piece in various concerts with his wife Caroline. It now achieves a steady sale from which I receive occasional minuscule royalties, and I derive much satisfaction that this fine work should have entered the public domain. I have played it myself with a friend, and it is technically quite difficult. This was only a small part of his output, and there are many more unpublished manuscripts which I have yet to go through.

He was active as a conductor and choral director, working as an assistant conductor at Glyndebourne before moving on to various other posts, including directing the Ludlow Choral Society and finding time for composition. It seems likely that if he had survived the war he would have gone on to achieve a successful and distinguished career as a musician. He seems to have combined the role of country squire with his musical life very successfully, and an eyewitness account has him strumming with his fingers a tricky technical passage for the piano, on the stock of his shotgun during a lull in a pheasant drive. I can readily identify with this, having found myself doing exactly the same!

By all accounts, my father was a man of happy and cheerful disposition, well liked, with a wide circle of friends. Bobbin Kennedy, a neighbour and an old girlfriend, recalls an occasion when he had just driven from London on a hot afternoon and finding all his family playing around in a boat on the lake in front of the house, ran gleefully down the lawn and flung himself into the lake, fully dressed, to cool off.

While my father was working at Glyndebourne, soon after the Christies opened their opera house there, he met Diana Moinet, who was secretary to John Christie. She was a Sussex girl having grown up nearby at Copthorne and been educated at Southover Manor in Lewes. Their shared love of music, among other things, drew them together and they were married in London on Wednesday November 10th 1937 at St Clement Danes Church in the Strand. Invitations to the wedding and reception afterwards were sent out by Mr and Mrs Cyril Moinet of Orchard House, Copthorne, Sussex. My mother, from a family group photograph taken when she was in her teens, was, in my opinion, clearly the best looking of the four daughters in her family.

The account of the wedding in the social columns of *The Times* described her as wearing

> *'a close-fitting gown of gold lamé, made with a high draped neckline and long sleeves. A short train was cut in one with the skirt and over it fell a longer train formed by her veil of old Limerick lace mounted on tulle. A halo of leaves surmounted the veil and she carried a sheaf of Auratum lilies, golden carnations and gerbera.'*

Although I am quite unfamiliar with these flowers and with the details of the style of the dress, it sounds impressive and, I imagine, expensive. She must have looked very striking and, indeed, her portrait by the society photographer, Lenare, shows an exceptionally pretty woman with remarkable eyes. She was close to the people at Glyndebourne and I still have a little silver box inscribed *To Diana on the occasion of her marriage, from a grateful Glyndebourne*.

Among those attending the service was Mr W.J. Backhouse, who came to feature prominently in the history

Childhood and Early Years

of our family after the war.

I was the first product of this happy union, and was born in Shropshire on February 13th 1939 at the Old Laundry, on the Ludlow Bridgnorth road, just one hundred yards from the gate of the front drive at Millichope. Seven months after my birth, war was declared and for the next five years the whole continent of Europe was locked in conflict. My father, aged 28, initially joined the King's Shropshire Light Infantry and later, for reasons that I have been unable to discover, the Royal Norfolk Regiment. For several years, he saw little if any action, which he found frustrating until, encouraged by his brother-in-law, David Haig Thomas, who by then had married his sister Nancy, he joined him in the Commandos, founded in 1940 by Winston Churchill to undertake special and generally more dangerous war-time operations.

It was as a member of Number 4 Commando that my father landed in Normandy, and was killed near Pegasus Bridge on July 11th 1944, just one month after the first wave of the Allied invasion on June 8th. David Haig Thomas was also killed in a separate action a few miles away.

It is very sad that I have so few direct personal accounts of my father's life but I do have a letter written by my mother to her younger sister, Penelope, on August 4th, less than a month after his death in 1944.

> *'I want you to know that now at last I have reached peace. You know me so well - my horrible failings to Frank in love and duty – and how many times since I have suppressed in shame - but never anything of course in comparison to my remorse since his death- when his full splendour*

shone so clearly- his courage- not only in his death- but in his sticking so uncomplainingly those long dreary lonely years of training and hanging about in loneliness and boredom. His natural instinct for good, kindness, courage and un-selfishness; always so gay and unself-conscious always ready to laugh at himself and the world. What I am and have been in comparison you know – and you can imagine how I suffered feeling myself so unworthy as if I could never hope to be reunited with him or God - but God has been very good to me I feel pardoned. I realise that Christ in his death atoned even for sins like mine and that only fresh sin will separate me from God and Frank. I am extremely comforted and supported now - I feel truly that the impossible may become or even have become possible - that communion of spirit, that feeling that Frank is with me.

He certainly is happy; he died fulfilled. There was no evil in him so he must be with God and his life must be my inspiration and his spirit will help me to do my best not to let him down.'

It is tragic to read this letter. I don't know why my mother felt so guilty and few people would judge that she should so feel, but she says some wonderful things about my father, which make me very proud. I think she must have felt that she should have seen more of him during the war years and perhaps tried to dissuade him from joining the Commandos, for which he must have been quite unsuited, having poor

Childhood and Early Years

eyesight and a generally unathletic physique. She may have tried, but he was not to be put off and wanted to play a proper, active part in the war. David Haig Thomas, who had encouraged him to join, was, by contrast, an Olympic oar, having represented his country in the Games of 1932, and an explorer with several expeditions to his credit, including an extensive trip to Greenland where he took my aunt Nancy on honeymoon. We used to tease my cousin Tony, their eldest son, that he was conceived in an igloo!

I have over the years paid several visits to my father's grave at the military cemetery at Ranville, about two miles from Pegasus Bridge. The cemeteries are beautifully maintained, and it is strangely moving to wander past the thousands of simple crosses, bearing the name and rank of each soldier. The age of each of the buried soldiers is recorded on the gravestone, and remarkable for me is the fact that my father was thirty-three, whereas the vast majority of his neighbours in the cemetery were in their early twenties. He should probably never have been accepted into the Commandos, although I am very proud of him for his courage and patriotism in joining such an elite unit.

I have also come into possession of an extraordinary document - a letter written by my father on 19 June 1944 shortly before his departure to France as a lieutenant and parachutist in Number 4 Commando, and about a fortnight after the Allied invasion of France on D- Day. The letter, written from the Commando Depot at Wrexham, not far away in North Wales, is addressed to me, his son Lindsay, and he had left instructions that in the event of his not returning from the war, I was to open it on my 13th birthday

A Shaky Start and a Lot of Luck

in 1952. Following the death of my grandfather, I cannot remember whether this letter was in fact shown to me and certainly I cannot recall having seen it before discovering it among a bundle of family papers when I was aged 73; so I finally read it - 60 years later!

It is a remarkable letter which I think is worth reprinting in full:

'My dear Lindsay,

If I am alive when you go to Eton you will never get this letter. I am writing it just in case I don't get back from the war for you must know that I was ordered to go to France last night and that I expect to go there and join a Commando tomorrow morning.

It will be very interesting that this war which to us is so vital, will be to you a chapter of history as the 1914-18 war was to us. What I hope will never happen is that your generation will grow cynical of the sentimental patriotism of its forebears: but that you will realise that a strong England, that is an England materially and emotionally strong, is the only way of ensuring a lasting peace.

At present wars seem to average out as events occurring to countries roughly every 25 years. Britain allowed herself to grow very weak, both morally and in armaments, at the beginning of this one and whatever may be the historical doctrine that you are now being taught, we were very nearly defeated in 1940. The only way to

Childhood and Early Years

avoid wars as I see it is by the production of a generation of true and honest men who will not tolerate a breakdown of truth and honesty in international dealings or business dealings any more than they would consider swindling their own neighbours and friends.

At the beginning of this war we seemed content to let our friends down right and left for the sake of a few more years of peace and security. As a result we lived in a fool's paradise and we have paid the price of spiritual weak mindedness by being involved in this terrible war which has separated your parents for the greater part of their married life, has robbed them of their home and has robbed me of the joys and privileges of seeing you grow up and develop.

To set against that war has undoubtedly strengthened my generation spiritually and mentally. We realise the value of an unselfish nationalistic pride of which perhaps we had grown cynical between the wars but deep down in our hearts we realise perhaps, although it has not come very strongly to the surface, the importance of spiritual and religious integrity.

At the time I am writing your mother is resorting to a spiritual quest and attacking her religious problems with an enthusiasm which only she can muster and which may have had and should have had, a tremendous influence on your life up to now; and which the Eton education which we have planned for you and which you have either had or are going to have, will or should have fostered greatly. I am sure that Christian ideals in personal and international relations are the only hopes of peace and although you may possibly be feeling that you have a lot of religion crammed down your throat, its ideals are worth following and studying even if as I hope is not the case, you find yourself unable to accept its divinity. Be strong-minded therefore and stick to the ideals you know to be right and be an influence to others. Remember, as perhaps I may not have remembered in the past as much as I should, that loyalty to a lost cause has its value. Stick to what you believe to be right. You may turn out to have made a mistake but at least you have gained the respect of both worlds.

I wonder how you are growing up and what are your interests and enthusiasms. I remember you as a very nice little boy with a nice fat little sister just ceasing to be a toddler. I wonder where you are living although I fear that there has not been enough money to keep on the lovely home we once had at Millichope. However let us hope you are still in the neighbourhood and the estate has not had to be sold.

At present time I am able to leave you in the position of being quite a lucky little boy with many kind people to bring you up in a part of the world I think and hope that your family are

Childhood and Early Years

respected and loved and every start in life that we can give you. Some of the advantages we are able to share. All the wise things that have been decided by the family should be done, have been your grandfather's decisions or decisions taken under his influence. I am sure you will learn to appreciate what a wise and good friend he is and that you learn to love him as we do. It's very sad that you never knew your grandmother (on my side). Your mother never knew her either because she was very wise most amusing and very attractive in middle age. She must have been very beautiful when young. The other day we found an old photograph of her at the wedding of your great uncle Bill with your great aunt Mimy. It is easy to see that with her natural wit combined with those looks and that character she could marry who she chose; and to show her discernment of the character of others she chose your grandfather and stuck to him and was engaged in the years before it was possible for them to marry and in the teeth of her own parents' opposition. With no money at all they started and I was born and later your aunt Nancy and I was given a splendid education for which they had to pinch and scrape; and whether it was worth spending all they spent on me and all they denied themselves for me I don't know. All I know is that they spent it and I am eternally grateful. Later your grandfather did well and achieved great distinction and when your grandmother came into Millichope was a happy time for us all. When she died a few years later it was very sad and I do not know how your grandfather got over it. He has found happiness since with the lady you now call grandmother and whom your mother and I have learned to love very much. I am sure you have learned to love her and admire the good looks she must still have in old age. Finally Lindsay comes the other blessing in your life for which I am entirely and completely responsible for after this I married your own mother and you and Sarah were born. Alas she is not physically strong and I'm afraid you will have to look after her a lot but by now I know that you are appreciating her central goodness and nobility of character. There may be times when headaches and weariness and ill-health make her a little cross but it is all over in a moment she is such an affectionate sensible person and she's made my life so happy.

Well old lad I hope you have not found this too boring and pompous. There is often a time when bright young men think their elders most awful asses and perhaps you do too and in this case you may be right. My excuse for writing is perhaps best expressed by TS Eliot "past experience in the meaning …is not the experience of one life only but of many generations" Therefore I have taken the liberty of giving you a little of

Childhood and Early Years

that on my generation and it is now time to finish. It is summer here and there is a lovely sunset over the Ruabon mountains (he writes from the Commando depot at Wrexham in North Wales) and I'm off tomorrow and I shall thoroughly enjoy every moment of it and have enjoyed every moment of my life so far and will enjoy many more moments with you and Sara and mummy and everybody. It is mummy who has had so much to bear and you must be very kind and gentle to her. Hug her and Sara for me and all the very best to yourself old boy

Your affectionate father, Frank Bury'

I was, of course, deeply moved by this letter, particularly after the passage of such a long time. I think this, together with the passage from my mother's letter to her sister Penelope, firmly establish that my father was a good man in every sense of the word, and both Sara and I feel desolated that we never knew him. Quite apart from the deeply-felt personal message that he is conveying, the strong moral and religious tone of both this and my mother's letter resonate strongly with my memories of youth and I think contrast pretty sharply with my experience nowadays. I don't think the modern generation would write in quite these terms, but the hardship, absences and deprivation of the war years ring vividly through the letters: our modern generation is luckier than perhaps they realise, not to have had to endure these things.

On a lighter note, I have been told that he was fairly chaotic in some of his habits and something of a sloppy dresser. A photograph survives of him in his army uniform sent to me by my cousin Tony Haig Thomas, which shows my father in his ill-fitting yeomanry uniform, wearing spectacles and a sheepish grin, with his cap having slipped to the back of his head; the breeches are very tight and the boots do not look particularly clean. Tony's comment reads:

> 'I enclose a photo of Uncle Frank which you might like to have. Confronted with such awesome military strength I am amazed that Adolf dared to start World War 2.'

Of my mother, I can remember little more. She was the second daughter of a family of four and was christened Diana Mary Moinet. The family lived in Sussex and I have a copy of her birth certificate upon which her father, John Cyril Moinet, describes his profession as a 'Brazilian merchant'. He was married to Mary, whose maiden name was Wilson. That family achieved considerable fame when one of their number, Edward, accompanied Scott to the South Pole and perished with him there. He was also a distinguished mountaineer and president of the Alpine Society. My mother's three sisters, Ann, Penelope and Jane, are long since dead; my mother was closest to Penelope with whom she corresponded frequently and referred to as *'her darling little puss'*.

My parents' early married years were spent at the Old Laundry, on the main road along the Corvedale. There she brought up my sister and me with brief, infrequent visits from my father, until his departure to France in 1944. Her photographs and a waist-length portrait in my possession show her to be a pretty woman with very expressive eyes.

Childhood and Early Years

As my father foresaw in his letter to me, she was not strong and was given to migraines and finally when she died in childbirth in 1947, one of the causes was, apparently, that she had a small heart.

I do remember an episode in Tunbridge Wells, at one of the homes of the Moinet family, which we used to visit from time to time. I slammed a car door shut, trapping her finger, which must have been extremely painful.

After my father's death, which caused her enormous anguish and sorrow as her letter shows, she did remarry after an interval of about a year. Her second husband, and my stepfather was a brother officer of my father's, called Hilary Lewis, and she writes a very illuminating letter to her sister Penelope about her feelings at the time. Unfortunately, the first three pages of the letter are missing but it continues...

> '.....*going to be married again. It is the last thing I ever expected to do and yet now I do feel instinctively that it is the natural thing to do. I wish I can see you to tell you he is a soldier friend of Frank's. They were together for a time before he became a Commando and he mentioned him often in his letters at that time. Later he dined with us once and almost immediately afterwards he was sent to India. He used to write to Frank pretty often and when Frank was killed he couldn't have been kinder and went on writing to me regularly although I had only met him the once. In August this year he came home unexpectedly on leave and we met again and*

from that time this seemed the inevitable end. He got a job in Germany on the control commission where he is now and is likely to be for some years to come. Lindsay and Gertrude (my grandparents) just met him in August and I think they liked him a lot and I hope they will a lot more when they really know him. Being stationed abroad makes it rather difficult but he comes home on leave on 16 January and then will come and stay with L and G and the announcement will be in the Times about the 19th. In all essentials he is so like Frank; in his outlook on values and unselfishness and kindness. I feel that with him one should be able to try and make the same sort of home and family life for the children that Frank and I had hoped to make. I feel it is a...... step to take having had such perfect happiness with Frank but I hope that when you know Hilary you will feel as happy about this as I do.

I do especially want you and Paul (Paul Goudime) to meet him and I wonder if we might drive over for a lunch with you?......"

This letter tells us something of my mother's feelings on remarrying and her early description of Hilary, my stepfather.

She refers to Hilary's posting in Germany as part of the British Army of Occupation, which I remember vividly. He was posted to start with in Husum, a village in Schleswig-Holstein on the North Sea coast, not far from the Danish border. We were billeted with a friendly family who had on display some beautiful models of ships, both warships and sailing ships, which the family had made. I also remember a predilection for lavatorial humour which seemed to be quite common in Germany; the lavatory door was adorned with pictures of bottoms on potties and related themes.

After a few months, we moved to Berlin, which was situated within the Russian zone of the country. The city of Berlin, however, was itself partitioned between the occupying powers with the British zone in the west, the French in the north west and the American in the south. The largest zone was the Russian, which included most of the centre of the city and most of the government buildings. I have recently seen some film footage taken in Berlin in 1945, a year before we arrived in 1946, which brings back vividly the state of the city at that time. The devastation was indescribable, with virtually every building in a state of collapse and rubble everywhere. The streets were eerily empty, with mainly military vehicles driving up and down and a few people scurrying about.

Through the Brandenburg Gate, the main street, Unter den Linden in the Russian Sector was dominated by an enormous poster of Stalin. Food queues were widespread as well as lines of people passing buckets of water and removing rubble. The city was unnaturally quiet. We had a reasonably comfortable house and I remember some American friends called Rankin, with whom we used to go boating from time to time, on one of the numerous lakes which lay within the British sector of Berlin. I must have shown an early liking for music because I remember accompanying a young German music tutor, Herr Borg, a good organist who took me to hear him playing on several organs in cathedrals and churches in Berlin, most of which were badly damaged. In retrospect, it is surprising that he managed to find any instruments in working condition. Sometimes he was playing the organ in churches without a roof!

My sister wrote a letter with a bit of help from her nanny Frau Gruber who she called Fräulein. She relates that she

> '….had a picnic on Saturday and the weather was very nice and daddy shot one duck and we played sardines; the next day daddy shot duck again and the Rankin's children came with us we went to Grunevaldsee and Zulu (our dog) brought the duck out of the water and daddy gave him a dog biscuit.'

Quite a gripping tale!

While we were living this agreeable existence, the population of Berlin was by and large close to starvation and, before long, Zulu disappeared, almost certainly to be eaten. Apparently, in the post-war years considerable amounts of food were shipped to Germany from Britain, which the UK could ill afford. Productive farmland in Germany hardly existed in 1946 and the devastation of the country, together with the cumulative effects of the Allied blockade and bombing, had brought about an acute shortage of food.

One development of lasting significance to my family did take place in Berlin. My mother had come to know an order of Catholic nuns who were distributing food and looking after starving people in the streets. She became greatly impressed with the dedication and wonderful work being carried out by the nuns and after a while she decided to convert to Catholicism. My mother and, indeed, my father, belonged to the Church of England having been married at St Clement Dane's in The Strand in London back in 1937, and the Burys as well as the Moinets were Church of England families. We, of course, were also converted and I have, with one or two wobbles, remained a Catholic ever since. My stepfather was the son of a Norfolk parson and he did not convert at the time but many years after my mother's death he became a Catholic.

In 1947, we all came home from Germany and it was shortly after this that she was due to go into hospital at Much Wenlock to give birth to her third child. The child was stillborn, and my mother died in hospital together with her child. That this came as a total shock to everyone is illustrated by a letter she wrote to Penelope in October 1947 two days before her death in hospital. It is a happy letter written by a young woman about to have her third child and full of routine plans and family news, with no apparent worries or forebodings.

> *'The baby I begin to think will never arrive-tho I am now quite enormous and it is definitely due today. Accordingly I am about to set off for Wenlock Hospital after an early tea with Doss. If it does not start tomorrow morning I am to have a medical induction but even that may not do the trick. It's horrid waiting especially as if I am late, I throw out Hilary's leave and I also suspect Dr Bigley will want my room. Still I can't grumble yet and I ought to be thankful that I've managed*

> to carry on to the end without mishap..............
> L writes most cheerfully from school and they say he seems well. I'm so terribly sorry darling that you came for such a wretched week here, a week when I was still so worried about little L and so undecided what course to take over big L (my grandfather) and the house."

So my mother died, and Sara and I became orphans.

As the letter relates, Sara and I were by then at boarding school. I was at Avisford, which was near Arundel in Sussex, and she at Les Oiseaux, a convent near Broadstairs in Kent which had been evacuated to Millichope during the war.

This is probably the time to recount my stepfather's unusual life and his influence on the upbringing of the two of us. Hilary Lewis was the son of a parson in Norfolk. At the outset of the war he had joined the Royal Norfolk Regiment, where he had come to know my father. He served for most of the war in India, from where he corresponded regularly, first with Frank and, after he was killed, with my mother. About a year later, a courtship began, carried on mostly by letters from India. Hilary came home on leave and proposed to my mother in the autumn of 1945 and they were married on May 4th 1946. He was a good-looking man, over six feet tall and, as I remember, a good shot. He was entirely conventional with beautiful manners, and an agreeable, friendly disposition.

Like many soldiers demobbed after the war, he had no job to go to and no training or qualifications for any trade or profession. Interestingly, he brought back from the army and his time on the Control Commission an admiration for the Germans and their determination to rebuild their country. After my father's death, my mother of course had been in the position of sole guardian and parent for Sara and me and we were the heirs to Millichope, a substantial country estate in Shropshire comprising some 3½ thousand acres, together with some land in Durham, both of which were held in trust. One obvious career for Hilary was to become a land agent where he might reasonably expect to take over the day-to-day management of the estate; he was encouraged in this aspiration by my grandfather, Lindsay Bury, and had set about taking a course in land agency.

Hilary was very much in love with my mother, and her death was a particularly appalling shock for him, since she died bearing his child, which had not survived either. He writes to my mother's younger sister Penelope on 25 October 1947, just after her death:

'My very dear Pen. Thank you so very much for your letter and for all you have done in these last miserable days. I still cannot see or think straight and feel as if everything has dropped out of the world. However, I am determined always to try and do whatever Diana would have wanted and I'm glad to have plenty of work to grasp onto....... Bless you Pen; for ever since I met Diana, you have always been there as a tower of strength. I feel, with you, that Diana may well have been spared illness later on and I am so glad that she was so happy up to the end and knew no pain and apprehension.'

A Shaky Start and a Lot of Luck

For the rest of his life, he kept photographs and letters of my mother in his wallet and her memory was indelibly printed on his mind. It would be surprising if he did not also feel some guilt, in that her pregnancy and resulting complications probably brought about her death. This love of her became partially manifest in an obsession with doing his duty by us, his stepchildren. I remember vividly receiving the news of my mother's death. I was at Avisford when I was summoned to the headmaster's study where Charles Jennings was waiting for me. 'Bury,' he said, 'I am afraid I have to tell you the saddest news you will probably ever hear in your life: your mother has died.'

Whereupon, he grabbed me and put my head under his arm and held me there. I was then able to cry unreservedly without feeling bad about it. Whatever the reason, I have never forgotten that moment and from then on I developed a dread of telegrams. My poor grandfather, whom I deeply loved, died just over four years later in 1952 and again the news came by telegram.

Although Hilary had met my grandfather, Lindsay Bury, in August 1946, he had never met Nancy, my father's sister, nor Penelope, my mother's younger and favourite sister, to whom the letters quoted above were addressed. The duty to look after us clearly pointed towards living in Shropshire, and he was much helped by the goodwill and assistance of my grandfather and his wife Gertrude.

Since Sara and I were both at boarding school, it undoubtedly brought the advantage that he could concentrate on his land agency studies without the day-to-day preoccupations of bringing up stepchildren, at least during term time. Sara and I were happy at our respective schools. In many ways, boarding school was our salvation, providing a secure base over what turned out to be a long period of emotional uncertainty. I remember there was a train which took an extraordinary cross-country route, picking up Sara from Ludlow and crawling its way along the south coast, to arrive about ten hours later at Broadstairs in Kent, without a single change. Hilary would occasionally visit us in term time and take us out to lunch in Brighton or some nearby town. It must have been a great relief that we were both happy, in good Catholic schools, so he didn't have to traipse all the way from Shropshire to the south coast to watch cricket matches, or become as closely involved in school life as is certainly the practice with most parents nowadays.

After a few years, he had a few girlfriends and I was never quite sure of the status of some of the nannies who looked after us. I remember one Miss Ward, whom we called Wardy. She was there for quite a few years and I remember her kissing us good night in a low-cut dress: she was a well-built woman and I enjoyed the experience. It is most unlikely that anything took place between Hilary and the nannies and, if it did, we certainly were unaware of it. More relevant was an American woman called Sheila, who turned up in an enormous Studebaker saloon, which could hardly fit into the garage, but this vast motorcar was quite enough to convince me that she should be his choice and, aged about eight, I lobbied hard for her but to no avail. He also quite fancied several of the prettier married women in Shropshire although again, I am sure nothing untoward took place.

In about 1950, however, he did bring home a woman called Anne Blackett Ord who came from a long-established Northumberland family with a large estate called Whitfield, including a renowned grouse moor on the headwaters of the river Tyne in the Pennines. She had been a Wren during the war and for a while had worked in a torpedo factory in Newcastle. She'd also nearly married a man called Matthew Ridley, who owned another large estate, Blagdon, on the edge of Newcastle. Their union would have been entirely suitable but it was not to be, and the engagement was broken off at the last minute, just before the ceremony.

At the time of meeting Hilary she must have been about 30. She was a tall woman with warm, brown eyes, and a full figure, voluptuous but not conventionally pretty. After a short while it became clear this was a relationship that was going to last. After quite an extended courtship they got married in 1953 and decided to go and live in Cumberland at a village called Newton Reigny, about three miles from Penrith. My grandfather who lived in Munslow, the nearest village to Millichope, and with whom we had been spending two weeks of each holidays, had died in 1952 and the obvious solution was for Sara and me to go and live in Cumberland, which we did.

We were not happy there; the weather was even worse than Shropshire and the train journeys up from both Eton and St Mary's Ascot (we had moved on to public schools by then) to Penrith seemed interminable. Cumberland was a long way from anywhere, and we failed to make any friends of our own age and felt cut off. Understandably Anne's

Childhood and Early Years

main interest lay in her own young family. She had by then had two children Caroline, who was born in Shropshire, and Michael. Many women marry men with children from an earlier marriage but Sara and I were not even Hilary's children! My main pleasure was to sneak off to Carlisle to a record shop, where I could buy the latest jazz recordings. Louis Armstrong and Humphrey Lyttleton did much to liven up some boring and usually wet days. One holiday, Sara came back from school in quarantine for mumps and Anne who was pregnant at the time, made her live in a specially hired caravan adjacent to the house, to which meals were passed through the kitchen window. From a medical point of view, the precautions were no doubt admirable but the whole arrangement seemed rather heartless.

Our lack of enthusiasm for Cumberland became known to our relations down south and, after two or three years, pressure began to build for us to spend part of the school holidays with my aunt Nancy, my father's sister who lived on Horsey Island in Essex, and part with my aunt Penelope and her husband, Stephen Nix, who had by then moved into my grandfather's former house in Munslow, near Millichope. This pressure Hilary vigorously resisted; as he saw it, he was our stepfather and guardian and we belonged with him. My aunt Penelope by then had become disillusioned with Hilary. She and Nancy were at one in wanting us to spend at least half the holidays in Shropshire or Essex, as opposed to Cumberland. The situation was aggravated by the fact that, following the death of my grandfather in 1952, trusteeship of the estate passed to my aunt Nancy, my father's sister, who was disinclined to delegate the day-to-day management of the estate to Hilary, whom she had begun to mistrust for some reason (which may have been why he decided to live in Cumberland). Hilary wrote a letter to Paul Goudime, whose support and assistance as my godfather was invoked by both parties:

> *'I came out of the Army to make a home for the children on the understanding from old Lindsay that I should be able to make a living by being made agent of the Durham and Shropshire properties when I passed my land agents exams. This has only been fulfilled in part. Like Diana I have always felt since I've been here that as long as one toed the line one was tied by silken cords which were not pulled.'*

He went on to complain that Nancy was increasingly demanding that Sara and I should spend half the holidays either with her on Horsey Island, or with Stephen and Penelope in Shropshire, whereas he saw it as his duty to bring us up with him; he owed it to my mother's memory. Hilary was becoming increasingly agitated by Nancy's pressure and, as early as January 1953, he took legal advice as to where he stood in the matter of custody of us children. He learned that having looked after us for seven years no other claimant would stand a chance but we, the children, would have to appear in court and the case would take at least three months. Not an appealing prospect as the trustees, Nancy and Eric Temple, a family friend and lawyer, might be disinclined to pay the fees!

In March 1953, Hilary received a letter from the family

solicitors, Sprott Stokes and Turnbull in Shrewsbury, informing him that my father's sister, Nancy, who by then was remarried to Jasper Backhouse, wished the children to stay with her or, alternatively, with Penelope Nix for approximately one half of each of the school holidays, and Mr Eric Temple, in his capacity as trustee, entirely agreed to this proposal.

Hilary's reaction was to write again to Paul Goudime, saying that he felt very strongly that *'if the children spent one half the holidays with us and half with their two relations they will not know whether they are coming or going.'* He also wrote to Temple, who was a solicitor as well as trustee, saying that the children must spend more than half of the school holidays with him as their guardian, who was responsible for their upbringing. He reiterated,

> *'…..I am the sole guardian of the children and that while I am perfectly agreeable to the children spending some time in each holidays with either or both of their aunts, this period must not exceed one quarter of each holidays, commencing this Easter and that Mrs Backhouse and Mrs Nix should regard themselves solely as their aunts not as guardians and do not in any way belittle my authority as guardian and stepfather or undermine the mutual affection between the children, my wife and myself.'*

There followed several more letters in which the lawyers suggested that the difference between a half and a quarter could be reconciled amicably and needn't mean resorting to the courts. Hilary, however, again stressed emphatically that he would not agree to any time longer than one quarter of the holidays.

The battle lines were now firmly drawn; an impasse had been reached. By now, however, I had been at Eton for several years and my housemaster, Oliver Van Oss, a formidable man and outstanding housemaster, entered the picture. Oliver was a larger-than-life character whose house was one of the most successful at Eton over a wide range of achievements. Although he was mainly interested in the academic and sporting successes of his house, he was also a perceptive man who took great trouble to understand and encourage all the boys in his charge. His assistance had already been sought by both my aunts and, indeed, by Hilary, both sides lobbying for him to talk to us and make a recommendation. One evening he summoned me to his study to give me his take on the situation. He spoke bluntly. 'Your stepfather is a well-meaning but not very bright man but undoubtedly he has your best interests at heart and he clearly perceives his duty to be in retaining guardianship until you reach maturity. Your aunts meanwhile have rather overplayed their hand in the way they have made their case but they are sincere in wanting the best for you, as indeed, is your stepfather. The answer is that you must decide now where you want to live. You cannot please both parties but you and your sister are quite old enough and well able to make this decision for yourselves.'

During the preceding months in 1955, Sara and I had discussed the situation and we were increasingly attracted by the idea of making a complete break, severing

Childhood and Early Years

connections with Cumberland and going to live on Horsey Island with my aunt Nancy. It was a tough decision, and it is fair to say that my sister was altogether more decided than I was on making the break, but we did it. I did feel guilty about leaving Hilary and hurting his feelings. I have a fragment of a letter, from a source I have been unable to discover, which says:

> *'... I have had a letter from Lindsay who writes sadly and says will I write and tell daddy how much he misses him and that he has not had a letter since October and it is very hard. He hopes he has made the right decision but it was a very hard one to make he asked me to write to cheer daddy up and tell him how much he loves him. I'm afraid he's worrying a good deal and evidently it is on his mind a lot; this will be so bad for his work and his happiness at Eton. I feel so sorry about it all. I have written to tell him I've written to daddy but afterwards thought it better to write to you. He mentions with great gratitude that you wrote him at Christmas and sent a very nice present.'*

I have no idea who wrote this and to whom it was sent.

Although, like Sara, I was pleased to leave Cumberland, I did feel bad about Hilary, and this continued for a few years, during which time complete silence reigned and no communication took place between us.

By this time, Hilary and Anne had two children of their own, Caroline and Michael, and he was working in a land agency practice where he had bought into a partnership, which became Musgrave and Lewis. I think that the disappearance of Sara and me from the household must have been in some ways a relief for Anne, who was then able to concentrate on bringing up her own children without the distraction of stepchildren, who were not even blood relations of her husband. I fear, however, that Hilary was bitterly hurt by our decision and regarded it in some way as a reflection on his role as stepfather and a failing in his duty to my mother's memory. Some years later we did renew contact; he attended my wedding and, in due course, my wife Sarah and I invited him and Anne to stay for the weekend at Millichope, where we were by then living. So after several years of separation, normal relations were resumed. By then I was aged 27 or so and the memory of our leaving Cumberland had abated. This was the first of several visits over the years paid to us in Shropshire by Hilary and Anne and, indeed, we used to call in on them quite regularly en route to Scotland. Reigny House, although not full of the happiest memories, was a convenient staging post, heading north up the M6 to Scotland where Sarah's family lived. Hilary had built up quite a good practice in Cumberland and was making a reasonable living as a land agent. He and Anne had friends in the county; he got a bit of shooting and was apparently quite content with his life there. It seemed to me a claustrophobic, provincial existence, from which I was pleased to have escaped, but he had settled there happily and begun to develop several new interests such as collecting bronzes and travelling to European capitals.

Much later, when I was in my 50s, I received an

Childhood and Early Years

extraordinary letter from Hilary saying that when he died he would like to be buried in my mother's grave in Munslow in Shropshire. The grave was a twin, providing for a spouse. My father was already buried in a military cemetery at Ranville in Normandy, so probably it was Hilary who made the decision on the twin grave before my mother's burial back in 1947. In any case, I found the request very difficult and sent him a letter saying that I could not think of anything more hurtful to Anne, to whom he been married for well over 30 years, while he was married to my mother for only eighteen months, a very long time ago. I realised by then that he was obsessed with her memory; her portrait dominated the dining room in Newton Reigny and her letters and most intimate possessions remained close to him for his entire life. I wrote back to express my misgivings about doing as he asked, chiefly on the grounds that it would cause enormous hurt to Anne, only to receive a further letter requesting strongly that I comply with his most heartfelt wish and that his wife was well aware of his intention.

At this, I sought the assistance of Michael, his son, saying that I felt disinclined to go along with it and that even if, as he said, Anne knew, it must cause her a great deal of hurt. I then received a letter from Anne:

'I hope you won't think it very odd of me to write, but there is a matter which I think we must settle before the inevitable happens. I think Hilary has said to you (and Michael) that he wishes to be buried with your mother at Munslow and that you intend to ignore this request. He

has said it forcefully to me as well, hoping that I would like to be beside them both eventually. I don't feel very happy about all this but find it difficult to tell Hilary so I now wonder whether burials are still possible in that part of the church yard anyhow? I write because Michael thought you did not know that I knew anything about all this. Perhaps your reply could be contained in a typewritten envelope.'

One evening in 1995 I got a telephone call from Anne saying that Hilary had died. Sarah and I hurried up to Cumberland where we went to a Catholic service in Penrith, which was then followed by a Church of England service and a cremation. Happily, we did resolve the problem of the burial by agreeing to divide the ashes which were to be scattered, half in a site in Cumberland and the other half on my mother's grave. The ashes destined for Shropshire were later delivered by Caroline, who leaned out of the window of a train in Wolverhampton, going from Cumberland down to Wiltshire where she then lived, and passed them to my chauffeur John Williams (I was off the road at the time), together with the portrait from the dining room at Newton Reigny. Half the ashes were duly scattered on my mother's grave.

A few days later I wrote a long letter to my stepmother, which covered a number of previously undiscussed topics which needed an airing. I told her that I was well aware of how difficult life had been for her inheriting two children who were no blood relations of her husband, and being lumbered with the responsibility of bringing them up

Childhood and Early Years

During all the period when we were in Shropshire and, subsequently in Cumberland, I considered that she and he had done a good job in bringing us up. I went on to say that I was well aware of his devotion to my mother's memory and his obsession with everything to do with her and how difficult that must have been. The letter continued in this vein for quite a while and I took a good deal of trouble with it. I was very pleased to receive a warm and thoughtful reply from her and, indeed, a further letter from Caroline who said that on reading the letter she felt much better about everything. So the ghosts were finally laid to rest.

In March 2017 Anne died. Sara and I went up to the Newcastle upon Tyne crematorium and found that virtually all the other mourners were from the Blackett Ord family. We were then surprised to hear from the vicar at the service, that Anne had always been obsessed with the death of her daughter, Joanna. Sara and I looked at each other in bewilderment; who was Joanna? During the journey back to lunch I asked this question and we learned that Joanna was the daughter born between Caroline and Michael and that she had died in a car crash. Her mother was at the wheel, driving back home from taking Caroline to a dancing class in Carlisle. Joanna was in the front seat, aged two years, sitting on her nanny's lap and Caroline was in the back of the car. The car collided with a tree and Joanna was killed instantly. It must have happened during the holidays and it now seems incredible that we were completely unaware of it. Sara vaguely remembers that we were prevented from going up to Cumberland for one term's holidays but it remains a mystery

A Shaky Start and a Lot of Luck

In any case, Caroline and, indeed, all the family were most friendly and welcoming to us and Caroline invited us to a family grouse shoot at Whitfield. We are now in regular contact and firm friends. The long saga has had a happy ending!

Chapter Three
Millichope and the Family

I've already referred to the Millichope Estate several times in this story and, since it has played an absolutely central role in my life, I should now describe it more fully.

Extending nowadays to about four and a half thousand acres, the estate lies in the middle of the Corvedale Valley in Shropshire, halfway between Ludlow and Bridgnorth. In my admittedly biased view it is the most beautiful estate in the most beautiful county in England. It spans the width of the valley between the long ridge of Wenlock Edge and the flanks of Brown Clee Hill, which are the two ranges of hills bordering the Corvedale. Half of the estate lies to the north-west of the main road, which runs down the middle of the valley. This half rises from the road up a long gentle slope ending on the ridge of Wenlock Edge, from which a steep escarpment falls away to the north-west. It is intersected by steep valleys, framed by hanging oak woods, mostly planted for shooting in the 19th century. Dramatic views abound and the estate has long been renowned as one of the finest shoots in Shropshire. The limestone ridge of the Wenlock Edge features some of the finest wildflower meadows anywhere in Britain, currently comprising about twenty-five acres but being extended to over sixty. There is very little topsoil so the limestone ridge is ideal for wildflowers. After a wonderful showing of cowslips in early May, during June and July the meadows glow in a kaleidoscope of ox-eye daisies, purple orchids, spotted orchids, birdsfoot trefoil, hawkweed, field scabious, with golden sheets of dyers greenweed and several rarer species such as the bee orchid, and one or two examples of the butterfly orchid. The view on a summer's evening from the meadows across the Corvedale valley to the Brown Clee Hill, with the profusion of colour from the wildflowers all around brings a feeling of joy and intense happiness in the beauty of nature. Everywhere on the north-west half of the estate, the contours offer dramatic and picturesque views.

By contrast, the half of the estate lying to the south-east of the main road is mostly flat and contains the best farmland; this half features the River Corve, with its tributary the Trow Brook and two wetlands, which are a magnet for wildfowl, with duck, snipe and lapwing, and otters. I once was privileged to see a pair of hobbies chasing dragonflies over the wetland. On the southern perimeter of the estate lies the village of Tugford, where Sarah and I now live, from where the terrain climbs steeply up into the foothills of the Clee Hill. The southern boundary consists of Harp Farm and its neighbouring woodland, already well elevated from the valley floor, which forms the hinge of the Corvedale valley. Standing on this vantage point, it is possible to view the valley broadening out towards Ludlow to the south-west and tapering back north-eastwards towards Bridgnorth and the source of the Corve, from which the Corvedale takes its name. From here there is a magnificent view across the valley to Millichope Park, the family house, surrounded by big trees and lying on the lower slopes of Wenlock Edge opposite.

Apart from the spectacular views to be found on the estate, there are some remarkable buildings. Several of the eight farmhouses have mediaeval origins, and three of the five historic churches in the Corvedale parish are situated within Millichope estate, Munslow, Tugford and Broadstone. Dominating the hamlet of Upper Millichope, towards the ridge of Wenlock Edge, is a 13th century building known as Forester's Lodge, thought to have been the lodge of the King's forester of the Long Forest, which in Norman times stretched from Buildwas on the river Severn to Craven Arms, and encompassed much of the Corvedale. The forester's job was to police the royal hunting preserves and to supply venison to the ppriory at Much Wenlock. Such were the severity and the unpopularity of the forest laws in medieval England that the forester needed a house which could be defended if necessary. Thus, the walls are six feet thick and it functioned as a castle keep or tower house, with the main living area at first floor level.

Prominent among all the buildings on the estate, however, is Millichope Park, which for forty-two years has been the family home for me, my wife and our two children, and is now lived in by my son, Frank and his family. The house is in the Greek revival style, a Grade II* listed building, designed by Edward Haycock, a leading early 19th century architect from Shrewsbury. The house was completed in 1840, three years after Victoria came to the throne but the style is neoclassical rather than Victorian. A *Country Life* issue dated 1975 featured four neo-classical houses built in the Greek revival style: The Grange in Hampshire, Belsay in Northumberland, Clytha in South Wales and Millichope, all considered prime examples of this period. Only the latter two are still lived in as private houses.

Millichope and the Family

The house stands in the middle of a substantial park of about 160 acres, extending from the River Corve to halfway up the slope of the Wenlock Edge behind the house. The significance of the park is recognised by its registration and Grade II* listing within the English Heritage Register of Parks and Gardens of Special Historical Interest, which includes only landscapes of national importance. Between the house and the park lie eleven acres of landscaped garden with a three acre lake in front of the house. The view from the house is incomparable; behind the lake and about fifty feet above it lies a knoll, on top of which is a temple built in 1763 to commemorate the death, during the Seven Years War, of two of the sons of Thomas More, the owner of Millichope at that time. This, together with the enormous cedar of Lebanon which towers over it, dominates the middle distance and, on the skyline, the eye is led up to the 540 metre summit of the Brown Clee Hill. My grandfather was fond of telling me that there is no higher hill to the east of the Brown Clee, before you reach the Ural Mountains in Russia. Thus the view has three tiers: a foreground with the big lawn leading down to the lake, a middle ground with the temple, the cedar and numerous tall trees and glades between ornamental plantings, leading up to the Brown Clee on the skyline in the distance.

To have inherited such a magnificent house and estate may seem an astonishing piece of good fortune and, indeed, for Sara and me it was. From the vantage point of sixty years later, with England bursting at the seams with people, and pressure for development at unprecedented levels, it seems incredible to be the owner of such a wonderful place. However, it's also true to say that some agonised decision-making and massive expenditure were needed to restore the house and revive the estate, but to my young mind it was already clear that Millichope had to be reclaimed and converted back to a private house at whatever cost; I would be the one to restore the family legacy.

A little family history is necessary to understand how it was that this magnificent property had remained intact, despite the lack of funds and hiatus in authority that followed the death in 1927 of my great grandfather, Henry John Beckwith, who had acquired the estate in 1896. The story of Millichope, however, goes back a long way before the Beckwith purchase. The estate was owned in the 18th century by the More family, who at one time owned several major houses in Shropshire including More, Linley, Larden, and Shipton as well as Millichope. Thomas de la More came over to England as one of the Conqueror's knights, dying at the Battle of Hastings. His family acquired property in the Corvedale in 1330. They were a prominent family in the area over centuries, and Robert More of Thonglands bought the Millichope Estate in 1544. A half-timbered hall was built about one hundred yards to the north east of the site of the present house sometime in the mid-16th century.

Thomas More plays an important part in the story because he it was who built the temple, which is so prominent a part of the view from the house. As an old man, he had to endure the loss of his three sons and the temple is a memorial to two of them who died in the Seven

Years War. The circumstances of their deaths are described on the cenotaph inside the temple. Major John More served under Sir William Draper in the expedition against the Philippines and was slain at the storming of Manila in October 1762 in his 42nd year. Apparently, hundreds of Spaniards and Indians were put to the sword but the Gazette of the day wrote:

> *'Our joy upon carrying the place was greatly clouded by the death of Major More who was transfixed by an arrow near the royal gate... universally lamented for his good qualities.'*

The other son, Leighton, was a spirited young lieutenant on board the Burford man-o'-war, who died of fatigue and illness in May 1777. He'd gone to sea aged eleven! Their father, overwhelmed by grief at the death of his three sons, his third son having also predeceased him, caused a series of monuments to be put up in their memory, the most prominent being the temple, designed by George Steuart, and completed in 1770, which predated the neo-classical Millichope Park by seventy years.

On Thomas's death in 1767, his surviving two daughters co-inherited. After a lengthy time in judicial proceedings his property was divided between the two sisters. It was Catherine who inherited Millichope Estate and she married her cousin Robert More in 1769. Robert was MP for Shrewsbury, where he also had a town house and was a prominent member of the Shropshire Enlightenment. An eminent and enthusiastic botanist and friend of Linnaeus, he was an early plant collector, who travelled widely. It is probable that several of the magnificent North American firs and pines, some of which now dominate the skyline at Millichope, were planted by him. The marriage of Robert and Catherine More was childless and, on her death in 1792 the estate passed to the Pemberton family. Robert Pemberton was a solicitor in Shrewsbury who was involved over a number of years in helping members of the More family. On his death in 1794, care of the estate passed to his eldest son, Thomas Pemberton, who was a solicitor in London but also a recorder of Much Wenlock, a Shropshire magistrate and chairman of Quarter Sessions. He was the guardian too, of his young nephew Robert Norgrave Pemberton, until the latter assumed responsibility for Millichope in 1832.

The Reverend Robert Norgrave Pemberton (usually referred to locally as Rev Norgrave) was a rich man, living at Church Stretton Rectory, and from 1841 at Millichope. Through his many land holdings, his income was estimated at some £5,000 a year. He set about increasing the size of the estate, notably with some purchases to the west around Munslow and to the north to include Munslow Common. Having inherited a maturing parkland landscape in the English style with grand classical garden structures, he probably felt that the three-hundred-year-old, half-timbered Millichope Hall was now no longer adequate for the rest of the site. He then set about building the present neoclassical house in the Greek Revivalist style, for which he commissioned Edward Haycock of Shrewsbury. Constructed in stone from the Grinshill quarry in North Shropshire, the house was well built from durable materials; indeed, this was a key factor in my decision

120 years later to restore the existing house rather than build a new one. It is astonishing to think that the enormous solid pillars on the front façade of the house were presumably lugged all the way from Grinshill, thirty miles away, and then sited on their base in three ten foot sections, through a system of carthorses and pulleys.

Rev Norgrave and his wife produced no heir and the estate passed to his distant cousin Charles Orlando Childe who, under the terms of Rev Norgrave's will, had to assume the additional name of Pemberton. He owned other estates in Shropshire, including Kinlet and, during the period of his ownership between 1849-1886, numerous innovative and dramatic enhancements to the landscape round the garden were carried out, notably cutting through the rock of the new front drive leading down to the Bridgnorth Ludlow road. A photograph also survives of a white five-arched wooden bridge across the lake, just below the temple. This structure did not remain there for long, presumably washed away by storm water. Charles Orlando's son, Charles Baldwyn Childe, inherited the estate from his father in 1883 but dropped the Pemberton name, and put it up for sale three years later. The estate failed to sell in 1883 and a tenancy ensued for a brief period until the sale to my great-grandfather, Henry John Beckwith, in 1886.

Beckwith was a landowner in Durham, and coal mining on his land was the source of his wealth. His family property was centred round Trimdon, in central County Durham in the middle of the Durham coalfield. There was also some property on the edge of Sunderland, with an

A Shaky Start and a Lot of Luck

imposing house called Silksworth, which for a long time was let to a Miss Doxford, presumably of the Doxford and Sunderland shipbuilding company. In 1896 H.J Beckwith, at the age of 56, acquired Millichope Estate in Shropshire.

I still possess in the library at Millichope four leather-bound volumes containing full particulars of all the estates in England that came onto the market at about that time. Although the estate failed to sell in 1883, I think it probable that he relied on these volumes for much of his information, before deciding to buy Millichope. The hyperbole and extravagant language of modern estate agents in describing property for sale was very much in evidence in the late 19th century!

> *'A most imposing structure, standing on an eminence, backed with magnificent forest trees; it is partly surrounded by a wide promenade terrace which runs the whole length of the building and from which the view is truly superb, looking across a sloping lawn, studded with rare shrubs; adorned with charming oriental lakes, a beautifully timbered park beyond and the picturesque Clee Hills rising above the lovely Corve Valley, the whole forming a most enchanting scene.'*

Apart from missing out the Temple this description is rather like mine.

The architecture of the house is described as being

> *'of a very artistic and chaste design and is constructed in a most substantial manner of Grinshill freestone and with its Grand Façade*

supported by fluted columns form a striking object that can be seen for a great distance.'

What, one wonders, constitutes a chaste design?

There follows a detailed description of the reception rooms, finishing up with reference to a well-ventilated dairy, bake house, brew house, cheese room and salting room; with details sufficient to satisfy the most avid Downton Abbey viewer. A further section contains a detailed description of the estate, with each field in each farm itemised, with the rent attaching thereto.

The estimated rental value of the mansion, woodlands and land in hand was put at £400 per annum while the estate, then comprising 3,131 acres, produced an income of £4,189. Notable among the particulars is the substantially larger number of small holdings and cottages on the estate in the 19th century. The trend, particularly since the last war, for farms to be grouped in larger units and the mechanisation and intensification of modern agriculture requiring far fewer farm workers, has resulted in rural areas becoming far more sparsely populated.

H J Beckwith seems to have been rather a formidable old man, owning two large estates and given to parsimony and righteous living. During the thirty years when he owned and lived at Millichope, he took the decision to disinherit his eldest son, Bill Beckwith.

I have never been able to discover why he took this step; one can imagine gambling debts, drunkenness and womanising perhaps; no doubt a disinclination to work, but there must have been plenty of Bertie Woosters around in the years before the First World War and, indeed, after,

A Shaky Start and a Lot of Luck

without such severe penalties being imposed by their fathers. Perhaps young Bill didn't have a Jeeves to keep him out of trouble! It has obviously turned out to my own great good fortune. I do recall once meeting a Beckwith descendant, who told me his grandfather was a hopeless case and happily, he didn't seem to bear a grudge. H.J.B also had a daughter Frances, who was referred to in my father's wartime letter to me as being a beautiful woman; it was she who married my grandfather, Lindsay Bury.

My grandfather's family home was originally Branksome Tower in Poole, now the site of a substantial hotel. He was one of three brothers, the youngest of whom, Ernest had a son Leslie, who emigrated to Australia in 1927, went into politics and became Minister of Defence in Robert Menzies' government, finishing up as Treasurer in the McMahon administration. He had four sons, three of whom I have met and the youngest, Nick, has become a close friend and lives at Vaucluse in Sydney, with his charming wife, Skaidritte.

Following several generations of Burys, my grandfather went to Eton where he achieved some success as a cricketer, among other things. About 40 years ago, I was a guest in the house of Maurice Bridgeman, then chairman of BP, who, when he heard my name recalled, 'Bury? Slow left-arm leg spin round the wicket.' That was my grandfather and they were in the Eton XI together a very long time ago. After leaving Cambridge, where he was at Trinity reading mechanical sciences, he was employed by the Egyptian Irrigation Service from 1904 to 1925, and, from 1919 to 1925, he was assistant inspector-general of irrigation in Egypt. Subsequently, he became Director of Irrigation and advisor to the Ministry of Communications and Works in Mesopotamia and Iraq. He then met and married Frances Beckwith. Her father, H.J Beckwith, was said to be a tough, miserly old boy; on his infrequent absences in London, the land agent had to account for every penny that his employer spent, which information was entered in spidery handwriting in the estate ledger.

When my grandfather showed interest in his daughter, H.J's initial reaction was not favourable but the couple persevered and, in due course, were allowed to marry. The disinheritance of Bill Beckwith was a great stroke of luck for the young couple. However, they spent a good deal of time looking for a house, usually accompanied by HJB, who was very negative about all the properties viewed, and did not let on that he had already decided to leave Millichope to them. He died eventually in 1927, following which Lindsay and Frances had twelve very happy years living there, as already attested by my father in his wartime letter to me. My grandfather decided to give up his career in the Middle East and returned to live in Shropshire, where he devoted himself to various unpaid activities in the county. These included Chairman of the Agnes Hunt Orthopaedic Hospital in Oswestry, board member of the Birmingham Regional Hospital Board, and Chairman of the Ludlow Division Conservative Association. Added to these were Member of the Shropshire County Council, chairman of the Ludlow Rural District Council, and chairman of the Ludlow Board of Magistrates. He had little time for anything else except his work in the county, all of which was unpaid. In the years after my father's death when we used to spend part of the holidays with him in Munslow, I used to accompany him to his meetings, driving round the county in an ancient Rolls Royce. Whenever possible, we listened to test cricket on the radio and I was quite happy to sit in the car while he went in for a meeting. In 1948 Bradman's all-conquering Australian side were sweeping away the English opposition and I remember the two of us listening with great gloom as Bradman and Arthur Morris accumulated 256 runs in a second wicket partnership in one of the test matches.

He was a wonderful companion and a dear man. By then, his first wife Frances had died and he had married Gertrude Worsley Worsick, whom I remember as being a frail but engaging woman. She was, though, quite demanding and I remember my ageing grandfather being regularly dispatched to various parts of the house to look for her spectacles or medicines. One Christmas, I was determined to get them both really special presents. I chose a bottle of Bulmer's Woodpecker cider for my grandfather; it came in a very large bottle and I thought that it would be well received. For Gertrude, I chose a book called *Unofficial Spy*. I forget the author, but the front cover showed a young blonde woman sprawled in a provocative pose, showing a lot of bosom: commonplace nowadays, but in the 1950s it seemed quite daring. My decision to purchase was clinched by the information on the front cover: "Two million copies sold." I felt that, with that many readers, it would be certain to please, and I was most deflated when she glanced at the cover with a pained expression and put it down as quickly as possible.

Millichope and the Family

At that time Sara and I were spending half of the holidays with Hilary at the Old Laundry and the other half with my grandparents, half a mile up the road at Millichope. I greatly loved my grandfather and was very upset when one day he told me that the average life span for men was three score years and ten. 'I am only two years off that Lindsay.' He did live for exactly two more years after that, and died in 1952 aged seventy.

The estate meanwhile had been put into a trust by old Beckwith, for the eldest son of Lindsay and Frances, my father Frank, and then upon his death in the war, it passed to a trust of which my sister Sara and I were equal beneficiaries. In my early youth, my grandfather was principal trustee and, after he died, this task was taken on by his daughter, Nancy, my father's only sister, who was married first to David Haig Thomas, killed within a month of my father in 1944 in Normandy, and then to Jasper Backhouse. My grandfather thus lost his only son and his only son-in-law and, as well as coping with this terrible loss, he had to make some difficult decisions about Millichope. Maybe if he had been possessed of a large fortune he might have followed the example of Thomas More and erected a memorial in the grounds. However, more mundane and pressing decisions had to be made.

Unsurprisingly, he thought that the days of big private houses were over and he decided to let the house and grounds. The first tenant was a school, run by an order of Roman Catholic nuns, the Canonesses of St Augustine, who had been evacuated from Westgate-on-Sea in Kent. They were running a boarding school for girls called Les

Oiseaux. The nuns were originally French and still had many French pupils. Shropshire, well away from German bombs, was seen as a safer refuge for girls from French families. The school's chaplain from 1930-38 had been Wilfred Upson, later the Abbot and Superior of Prinknash Abbey. He kept up his association with the school and this no doubt explains why Prinknash rented Millichope after the departure of the nuns in August 1945. The monks remained there until 1947. It was at Les Oiseaux that my education commenced and I was the only boy pupil amid the Catholic girls at the school for a short period during the war.

The next tenant of the house and grounds was the Shropshire County Council, who established an experimental secondary modern boarding school there, with a lease that lasted from 1948-1962 when I reached the age of 22. The school children ranged all over the house and grounds and made full use of them. The headmaster, a Mr Schulz, was fond of shooting rabbits with a 2.2 rifle and in those years going for a walk there could be quite hazardous. However, to judge from the reminiscences I have heard over the years from numerous former pupils revisiting Millichope, they had a great time and for many years I received visits from old boys, who took much delight in telling me where their dormitories and classrooms used to be.

Those immediate post-war years were a time of rationing and hardship. Now in the early 21st century frequent, indeed, monotonous use is made of the word 'austerity'. We certainly had our fill of the real thing in the early fifties,

Millichope and the Family

when the term really meant something. Great Britain was nearly bankrupted by the war, and it was not until the Marshall Plan and the resulting boost to the European economies, that the long period of post-war austerity began to lift. I remember rationing and have a vivid memory of the arrival of the first shipments of bananas, which seemed unbelievably exotic. Eventually people could afford new clothes and have a few holidays. Large country houses, however, were being pulled down at the rate of one every five days. It was largely due to my grandfather's decision to find a tenant for the house, keeping it heated and in good repair, that saved Millichope for another generation. But immediately after leaving Cambridge, aged twenty-one, I finally had to come to terms with what to do about the house.

Chapter Four
Eton and Teenage Years

The years leading up to my majority I'd spent at Eton and Cambridge. I arrived at Eton after leaving Avisford in 1952. Both my father and grandfather were old Etonians. My grandfather was then still alive and, notwithstanding the fact that Eton was not a Catholic school, my stepfather accepted that it was where I should go. Eton is one of the finest schools in the world and I was privileged to go there. It was a big jump from prep school, where I'd become a big fish in a small pond, to a vast school with about 1,200 boys, grouped into more than 20 separate houses, and I retain some vivid first impressions.

We had to wear a somewhat preposterous suit with a black tailcoat, striped trousers and white tie. The suits were made by a handful of traditional tailors with double-barrelled names, Denman & Goddard, New & Lingwood, Welsh & Jefferies, Tom Brown and several other venerable establishments who were only too happy to invoice the young gentlemen for the cost of these strange garments. Being black, the coats were not good at absorbing stains, of which there were many, and at frequent intervals we used to fling them onto a large shelf, from where they were removed and returned a few days later, duly cleaned and pressed. We each had our own room, which was a big step up from the prep school dormitory that I was used to. One custom we had to come to terms with was fagging. Each of the junior members of the house was allocated to one of the prefects or members of the 'library', who, when he wanted something, would yell 'B-o-o-o-o-oy' and we all had to go rushing off to see what he wanted, which normally meant running errands. Each house consisted of about sixty boys and I was lucky to have as housemaster, Oliver van Oss, one of Eton's most distinguished masters who went on to become headmaster of Charterhouse many years after I left.

Van Oss was a big, corpulent and red-faced man with an avuncular manner, a sharp eye and quick tongue. A shrewd judge of character, he took considerable trouble to develop and encourage the boys in his charge. If he was a little too inclined to cultivate lords and ladies and the upper echelons of society among the parents, it was a pardonable fault and common to many schoolmasters. His house was regarded as one of the best in the school and I owe him a great deal; as I also mentioned earlier, it was he who helped me make the vital decision about where Sara and I were to spend our holidays, and later on he fast-tracked me into Cambridge.

After an initial phase when I found the place huge and bewildering, I settled down well and greatly enjoyed my first few years. Van Oss's house was situated up a passage in a building called Jourdelay's, close to Eton High Street. Each house was headed up by a 'library' consisting of the house prefects who were primarily responsible for discipline. In addition to fagging, there were quite frequent beatings, which could be painful. Thus I remember being beaten twice at Van Oss's house, once by Jeremy Pinkney, and once by the present Lord Cadogan, then Charles Chelsea. My offence on one occasion had been to throw mud out of my window box at the head of a boy entering the house, who I thought to be a classmate but turned out to be David Pryce Jones, a 'library' member and now a distinguished figure in the literary world. He looked up, identified the thrower and I knew I was in trouble. Retribution followed that evening. I richly deserved to be beaten, being quite obnoxious and pleased with myself, and I received twelve strokes of a whalebone cane, which was an undeniably painful experience. The spectacle was watched by the other members of the library whose chairs were arranged in a semicircle around the victim's chair. The main thing to be said in defence of a beating is that it was all over quickly. The offence having been committed, the captain of the house had to get permission from Van Oss and punishment was administered the same day. In retrospect, I think there is a lot to be said for it, although I can imagine that it wouldn't be suitable for all boys. The alternative was writing out a *Georgic* by Virgil. At about 1,000 lines, this task took an eternity and was unbelievably tedious as well as ruinous to handwriting. I preferred the beatings.

Work was quite demanding and standards were generally high; each day 'early school' began at 7:30 am and lasted three quarters of an hour, followed by a return to Jourdelay's for breakfast. If the master was more than twenty minutes late for his class, the boys had a 'run' which meant that they could skip the class and return to their house early for breakfast. I remember one particular maths master, called Herbert, who was often late. He was a housemaster and from our classroom we could see into his bedroom; he

Eton and Teenage Years

liked an early-morning cigarette and would light up first thing when he woke up. We would watch him sitting on the edge of his bed in his underpants, puffing away before climbing into his clothes, while we looked anxiously at our watches, speculating whether he would make it on time. I recall at least two occasions when he did not and we had a run. In fact, he was a good maths master and we learnt probably more during his truncated lessons than in the full measure offered by some of his colleagues.

I did tolerably well during my first three years, got reasonable reports and made friends who have remained with me all my life. Van Oss's house succeeded in winning the house field game competition in 1954, for which I was awarded my colours but, in other games, notably cricket, where I was in the 1st XI at Avisford, my standard fell away and I didn't get into any of the top sides in my last two years. I entered for the school boxing as a middleweight, got through three rounds and was due to fight Robin Peat in the semi-finals. He had to withdraw due to flu, so I found myself, to my horror, in the final, destined to fight against Michael Hare, now Lord Blakenham, ex-chairman of Pearson group as well as the RSPB. Michael was captain of boxing and one of the best fighters that Eton has ever produced. Meeting him fifty years later, I was struck by his powerful shoulders and neck muscles, clutching a drink at a cocktail party. The school gymnasium was packed with several hundred boys who had come to see the demolition of Bury. Anyhow, I survived until the second round when, after a minute, the fight was stopped and I was sent to my corner, in no way hurt.

A Shaky Start and a Lot of Luck

I do think it is ridiculous that amateur boxing has been discontinued in all major schools. A contest of only three rounds, presided over by a good referee, should not result in serious injuries. It also demands a high degree of fitness, skill and a measure of courage, which surely is beneficial to a young man. I am interested that rugby, which we also played at Eton, is now blamed for some spinal injuries with the risk of paraplegia, and the talk now is of having the rules governing tackling, modified. I have always thought it more likely that you'll get hurt on the rugby field than in the boxing ring.

Generally, my progress at games was not spectacular but I did begin to devote quite a bit of time to music and particularly the piano. Looking back, I was wretchedly badly taught, with plenty of encouragement but never any emphasis on being made to practise properly and I skated through pieces with many sloppy mistakes. I did, however, discover quite a wide range of the piano repertoire, which laid down the foundations for a lifetime's love of music. I entered for the Drummond Cory piano competition and came third, playing Debussy's *La Cathedrale Engloutie*. I also used to turn up for some of the school concerts. These often featured well known virtuosi, but there were some home-grown performances. I still remember a German teacher called Howarth, who was an enthusiastic singer particularly of German *lieder*. His appearance was a bit unfortunate – of medium height with a red face, attention was immediately drawn to his hair which was cut very short and stood up vertically. It was also covered in what looked like sweat but was probably hair oil or some other preparation from the trichologist. We called him Treaclebush and during some of the more emotionally charged passages of the *lieder,* it was difficult not to get the giggles.

I also began to do better academically and came third in the Rosebery Prize, which was the competition for writing historical essays. At the age of 17, however, I'd had enough of school and wanted to move on. I was impatient to discover more about life so, when Oliver van Oss told me that Trinity College Cambridge had offered me an immediate place, I jumped at it. As noted earlier, Trinity had an arrangement with Eton whereby they would take three boys each year, purely on the recommendation of the school, dispensing with the requirement to take any exam whatever. It would mean postponing national service, which did not altogether please me because I much enjoyed the Corps at Eton, which took us to a summer camp where we played soldiers for two weeks. I was nonetheless persuaded by van Oss that it was too good an opportunity to miss, and so to Cambridge I went.

I have already covered the Cambridge years; the next chapter covers my first attempt to earn a living!

Chapter Five
Horsey Island and My First Job

During the time I was at Eton, my sister Sara and I lived first in Shropshire, then after my stepfather's marriage, in Cumberland and, from 1954 onward, on Horsey Island, the home of my aunt Nancy, my father's sister. I've already mentioned Nancy, when Sara and I made the decision to leave Cumberland and go to live with her and her family on Horsey Island. She now takes centre stage in this narrative. She had already led an unconventional and remarkable life. She married David Haig Thomas who, besides being an outstanding oarsman and gaining a blue at Cambridge, was also an explorer, and in their early married years they went on an expedition to Greenland. Just before the war, they bought Horsey Island, an island farm in the middle of the Naze, a backwater situated off the north-eastern coast of Essex between Harwich and Walton. Three hundred and fifty acres in size within the sea walls and surrounded by thousands of acres of saltings, the road track to the farm is only accessible twice every twenty four hours for four hours at a stretch: the rest of the time it is covered by sea. Although surrounded by towns on the mainland, Horsey is a completely wild place; the size of the island is dwarfed by the surrounding marsh, not only adjoining Horsey, but also Skippers, Hedgend and Bramble islands, all uninhabited except for tens of thousands of ducks, geese and wading birds. The silhouette of the island features on the front cover of the novel *Secret Water* by Arthur Ransome, and it was well known to Peter Scott, the great naturalist,

Horsey Island and My First Job

a friend of Nancy's, who painted a mural of a skein of geese flying across the ceiling of the old kitchen in the farmhouse. Horsey is now a nature reserve of national importance, host to vast numbers of Brent geese, with avocets (recently reintroduced by my cousin Joe Backhouse), as well as every kind of wader and duck.

Nancy lost her husband David during the war in Normandy, shortly after losing her only brother, my father, in the Allied landings in 1944. In fact, David was listed as missing and I believe no record of his death survives. Thus Nancy and her father, my grandfather, lost respectively a brother and a husband, and a son and son-in-law, within a fortnight of each other. She then lived alone on Horsey Island, somehow managing to run the farm and keep body and soul together on very little money. She became a good shot, and accounted for quite a number of flighting duck during the war years, to help feed her young family. I possess a large number of wonderful letters to her father in which she would bring him up to date on the day-to-day details of island life. They are full of vivid description, together with wry, ironic comments, which make absorbing reading; these letters must have been a lifeline to the old man in his grief. Since her childhood at Millichope, she had loved birds and animals; she had even kept a pet badger with some ducks, which waddled in and out of the large grand dining room. When I was living at Horsey Island, I particularly remember the swallows' nests immediately above the kitchen table where we ate every meal. Under no circumstances were they to be disturbed! In midsummer, there would be clouds of wasps in the kitchen. Nancy wouldn't turn a hair though, when they became too tiresome, Jasper, her husband, his face encircled by wasps, would crush a few with his forefinger. I never remember anybody being stung! Tough, practical and resilient, she had kind blue eyes with a magnetic personality and everybody who met her, came under her spell.

Nancy had two sons by her first husband, David Haig Thomas. Tony and David were my contemporaries at Eton, and we grew up together in our teenage years. After the war, she married Jasper Backhouse who came from an East Anglian banking family. Jasper had had a tough war in the Middle East and Italy. Having been very much a debonair young man about town in the 1930s, after the war he completely altered course with marriage to Nancy, happily settling down to life as a farmer on Horsey Island. He and Nancy were wonderful parents to us and we were very happy there, growing up with the two Haig Thomas boys and the three Backhouse children, Mary, Hannah and Joe. Tony was passionate about model aeroplanes and under his careful tuition I built one. It had a minute engine and one day I launched it on its maiden flight down the house field at Horsey. Imagine my horror when, after a very successful flight of several hundred yards, it landed and a large sow ambled up and proceeded to eat it, engine and all, before I could stop her. The sow was called Aunt Petitoes. We also became rivals in a different sphere. Placido, the Italian farm-worker on the island, had a pretty daughter called Rosalba. She was dark-haired, nubile and very desirable and when we all played sardines, Tony and

Horsey Island and My First Job

I would hide in different haystacks and pray that Rosalba would be the first to find us. For a while we became Essex boys and girls; sometimes coming home late at night after parties on the mainland, Tony and I would have to wade through the sea up to our waists to get home.

I loved Horsey Island, as everybody does, and absorbed a great deal from Jasper and Nancy, who had a totally different approach to life to that which prevailed in Cumberland. In later years, when I was building up ACT, Jasper took an intense interest and did everything he could to inform himself about the computer industry. I think his pleasure in our success was matched by my pride in having put to good use some of the many lessons in life that he and Nancy taught me. Sadly, Jasper was a chain smoker and died of emphysema, and Nancy once again became a widow. Sarah and I took her on a safari trip to Tanzania and Botswana on my fiftieth birthday. She took huge pleasure in the magnificent wildlife of the Serengeti, but she did try and restrain our safari guide from driving the vehicle too close to the wildebeest mothers and calves. She didn't want them to get separated!

While I was up at Cambridge, and during my early years in the City, I became increasingly conscious of the more conventional and less complicated upbringing of some of my Etonian friends. I had friends whose fathers were mostly businessmen or bankers and I was regularly invited from Eton, and later Cambridge for weekends at their homes. David Cobbold, son of Kim Cobbold, Governor of the Bank of England, had been in Van Oss's house and was a close friend, particularly when we both went to

A Shaky Start and a Lot of Luck

Cambridge and I regularly stayed at Knebworth, his family home. Julian Sheffield, whose father John Sheffield was chairman of Portals, the banknote paper-making company, lived at Laverstoke in Hampshire, surrounded by a beautiful estate on the River Test, with a renowned partridge shoot. Julian also went on to Cambridge and has remained a friend all my life; indeed, I later served as a director of Portals for 23 years.

The Norman family also played an important part in my Eton life. Bryan Norman was the son of Mark Norman, a director of Lazard bank in the City, as well as Gallaher, and several other major companies. They lived in a lovely house at Much Hadham in Hertfordshire. Bryan's great uncle was Montagu Norman, Governor of the Bank of England in the interwar years. I spent many happy weekends at Much Hadham as well as at St Clere in Kent, which was the home of Bryan's cousin, Ronnie. There were others, notably the Palmer Tomkinson family, and Simon Cairns, whose father was an admiral and finished up as Marshal of the Diplomatic Corps, with a flat in St James's Palace. The influence of these various households had a great effect on me. I noted that the head of the family seemed to have reached considerable eminence in large, well-established companies and each family seemed happy, relaxed and confident and to be well-positioned to cope with life. I felt that, after all the insecurities of my childhood, notwithstanding the happy holidays we were now spending with Nancy and Jasper on Horsey Island, I wished my life to follow the same pattern, which would definitely mean achieving success in business. Van Oss

Horsey Island and My First Job

had advised me against a life of managing my family estate in Shropshire, for reasons which were not entirely clear to me at the time, but I think he was right. Even before going up to university I had decided that I was going into business.

This ambition remained throughout my Cambridge years and, on leaving university, I started seriously looking for a job. I was clear that I wanted to be a merchant banker; merchant bankers seemed to straddle the top jobs in industry as well as the City, and Schroders was my first choice. In fact, I was offered two other jobs; one by John Sheffield who, in addition to his career at Portals, was also chairman of an engineering company in the West Midlands called Horsley Bridge and Thomas Pigott. I think he felt that since I was based in Shropshire, a job in the Midlands would fit in well with my life there. Mark Norman also offered me a job at Lazard, which was more tempting because I didn't want to bury myself in Shropshire at that stage of my life. However, I was set on Schroders, particularly as I had good contacts there, notably Jock Backhouse, Jasper Backhouse's elder brother, who was a director.

Schroders, however, was full up and not recruiting; there was no place for me and I was a bit despondent. It was about this time, however, that David Cobbold invited me to spend the weekend at Knebworth, and Kim Cobbold, his father, asked me what I was doing about getting a job. I gave him a full account of my searches and he muttered that he would write to Mr Abel Smith, one of the Schroder directors, to see what could be done. Shortly afterwards, I was invited to attend an interview, where Gordon

A Shaky Start and a Lot of Luck

Richardson, the then chairman (later himself to be Governor of the Bank of England) was present. Presumably, he was curious to see this youth who Cobbold had recommended! I was duly offered a job with a starting salary of £500 a year, working at No 145 Leadenhall Street in the City of London, with a desk in the banking hall. Thus, in 1960, I started my business career.

Meanwhile, I was still spending part of the holidays on Horsey Island but on coming down from Cambridge I took up residence in the Old Laundry, which was the house at the end of the front drive at Millichope, where my parents had lived during the war, and where Sara and I had lived with Hilary in the post-war years. The Laundry was a lovely old limestone house with a view over the Clee Hill and a lawn stretching down to the Corve River, with a beautiful weeping willow tree, underneath which I had spent some early years in my pram! There is a well-proportioned, quite large south-facing drawing room. This is where my father's piano used to stand, together with a huge collection of 78 rpm gramophone records: Schnabel, Gieseking, Toscanini and Caruso were all there. They weren't often played, however, because by the mid-fifties, 45 rpm and then 33 rpm vinyl records had arrived with much better sound quality.

I remember with shame a terrible afternoon up the Deans, a valley behind the village of Munslow, when some friends and I used the 78s as clay pigeons and shot the lot. It was a display of pure vandalism, the memory of which still makes me shudder. Another vivid memory from those days was coming down to breakfast with Edward Adeane, another friend from Eton and Cambridge who was staying, and our old gardener Billy James shuffled in and said, 'Bad business in America'

'WHAT!' I exclaimed, because I had never heard Billy talk about anywhere beyond Craven Arms, let alone America.

Sure enough it was to tell us about the assassination of Kennedy in 1963. Everybody remembers the moment when they first heard about the assassination of Kennedy; Edward and I were no exception.

A disadvantage of the Old Laundry was the road running past the house. In those days, the traffic along the main Corvedale Road, the B4368, was not at all heavy and it had not yet become the main artery connecting east and west Shropshire, which has made it such a nightmare today. Traffic has certainly ruined the Old Laundry; there is nowhere even to take the dog for a walk! I had by then acquired a car, a Hillman Imp (which I crashed within weeks of taking delivery), and when I was at Cambridge and subsequently, working in London, I often brought friends up to stay for weekends.

One major preoccupation throughout my later years at Cambridge and, indeed, through my twenties, was what to do about Millichope. When I reached the age of twenty-one in 1960, the Shropshire County Council's lease on the building expired and I decided not to renew it because, before too long, I wanted to live there myself. The house was enormous and I hadn't the first idea of what to do about it, and my decision to discontinue the lease meant that it remained empty for another seven years. I have vivid memories of sleepless nights, trying to decide how to keep the structure intact until its future seemed clearer. I had discontinued the lease because I was determined to live at least on the site of the house with no idea what sort of house should replace it. But buildings don't like being empty and the condition of the house was deteriorating. I was only in my early twenties, unmarried and I had not got the money to rebuild or modernise the house even if I knew what to do. However I was certainly not short of advice.

'You'll never be able to live there,' said one friend.

'It's just too big. It will cost a fortune to keep it up and it's getting damp,' said another.

'It's just not suitable for modern living. Heating it alone will be a nightmare.'

This depressing stuff came mostly from the older generation, but my contemporaries were no more hopeful.

Nobody thought it was going to be possible to live there and, thinking forward to when I might get married, I doubted that any young wife would want to live there. Usually, weekends would form a pattern, with tennis in the summer and a bit of shooting in the winter on Saturdays, followed by regular visits on a Sunday morning to the house at Millichope. We would walk up the front drive and wander around the large daunting, cold building. As the years went by, I began to notice damp stains on the walls where water was getting in. After the school had left, I couldn't let it again on a short lease and never really tried because I felt that it wouldn't be long before work started on some sort of conversion. It was a big headache and

Horsey Island and My First Job

I didn't know what to do.

Looking back, the most difficult period in my life was undoubtedly that period in my early twenties, when I was starting my career in Schroders, worrying about Millichope, and looking for a suitable girlfriend, possibly to marry, and, at the same time, for an unsuitable girlfriend with whom to have a bit of fun. It was interesting that I made this distinction, and thought it somehow wasn't right to have the fun with someone you proposed to marry! Ten years at all-male educational establishments hadn't improved one's knowledge of these matters. I was, indeed, very innocent and I regret to say that, although living in London, the swinging 60s more or less passed me by.

The nearest we came to it was when Robert Skepper and I were sharing a minute flat on a top floor in Curzon Place, Mayfair. Our next door neighbour in the flat immediately opposite was Vidal Sassoon, then London's top hairdresser. One day he approached me. 'Lindsay can I borrow your flat for a party? We are not all going to fit in here.'

I agreed, and it was a memorable evening. Vidal's flat was packed with various actors and show business characters. I remember Stanley Baker, Albert Finney, Jill Bennett, Jean Shrimpton and David Bailey, among many others. The Ray Charles number *'Hit the Road Jack'* had just come out and it was played again and again and again and again: *'Hit the Road Jack, and doncha come back no more, no more, no more, no more....'*

Everybody was jammed in shoulder to shoulder and jumping up and down and yelling their heads off. The food was laid out in my flat and the mess afterwards was indescribable. We nearly had to move in with two Danish tarts who lived in the third flat on the same floor. It was undeniably a good party.

Interestingly, our telephone number at the flat was Grosvenor 8000 and that of the Dorchester Hotel was Mayfair 8000. We got a fair number of calls from guests of the Dorchester reserving rooms, or tables at the restaurant. Robert much enjoyed taking these calls and made some interesting reservations and assignments for very puzzled clients.

I did, however, feel very insecure and would have liked to emulate several of my friends, who were getting married and settling down in attractive, easy-to-manage houses in the home counties, with settled families and what seemed good jobs. It was difficult to take friends back to Horsey Island; there was not really enough room and, although I loved going there and have continued to love going there all my life, it was less than ideal for entertaining. Besides which, the centre of gravity of my life had moved to Shropshire. So most of my socialising at weekends was done at the Old Laundry, which was home, but without the support of a family, other than my sister Sara, who was anyway having a few struggles of her own at that time. We had a devoted housekeeper called Muriel Allen, who would cook at weekends and make the beds and do the housekeeping. Scandinavian orange cream was her speciality pudding. The top half consisted of a mousse, coloured light orange, which was fine but the bottom half was an orange coloured sludge which hadn't set properly.

Horsey Island and My First Job

We thought it was delicious and several of my friends still remember it. She was wonderful and very understanding; the young gentlemen and their girlfriends, not to mention their host, would leave the house in a terrible mess when leaving to go back to London on Sunday afternoons. It would then take her till Wednesday to clear up, and if we were coming back the following weekend, she needed at least two days to get the house ready so this meant starting preparing on Thursday! I'm happy to say she is still alive and living in Ludlow and we keep in regular touch sixty years later.

Meanwhile, I was beginning to settle into the job at Schroders. I started at 145 Leadenhall Street in the City of London and I was working in the banking hall. One of my tasks was to count cheques with the aid of a rubber finger thimble called a Fingerit. The names of the banks on the cheques were usually prominent private German banks, with names such as Hugo Stinnes, Brinkman Wirtz, Bankhaus Friedrich Simon, Sal Oppenheim, and many others which I have since forgotten. I also had to write out the narrative on the cheques, and was mortified on being pulled up one day and told I did not know how to spell forty. I had written down 'fourty'! I did reflect that my 2:1 history degree, of which I was still very proud, was not proving very useful. Playing around with the Fingerit and writing out cheques was not very intellectually demanding and, from time to time, I felt I wasn't really learning anything. With my salary of £500 a year and hours of 9am to 5pm, there was plenty of time to use the telephone to organise the evening socials. I did, however, get on well

A Shaky Start and a Lot of Luck

with my working colleagues, most of whom came from the outer eastern suburbs of London in Essex. Despite no doubt being perceived as a toff, I had a good store of vulgar limericks and jokes which went down well.

After I'd been at Schroders for about three years, they took over the firm of J. Helbert Wagg, which was primarily an investment management house. I was moved over to Wagg's and started out in private portfolio management and from then on the stock market became my main focus. To start with I was producing valuations for our clients, many of whom were well-known figures, and it was interesting to see how much, or how little, money they had. I was soon in trouble in this department. One of the main board directors of Schroders had invested in a share called EV Industrials. This had proved a disaster and the company went bankrupt. I happened to know this director's daughter quite well, as she had recently married one of my close friends. Nobody at the office had particularly emphasised that clients' private financial affairs were a matter of the strictest confidence, although of course I should have known. She and her husband invited me to supper and I was soon gleefully recounting the sad fate of her father's investment in EV Industrials. I then went home and thought no more about it. However, about a week later I was summoned by David Ogilvy and Ashley Ponsonby, who were in charge of the investment department, to a meeting at which I was told that they were reasonably certain that I had been extremely indiscreet and divulged the private dealings of one of the directors. After some initial confusion, I realised that they

Horsey Island and My First Job

must be referring to EV Industrials and I confessed to the indiscretion. Ogilvy then said that I should go and see the director concerned and apologise and that my fate at the bank would be in his hands. This I did a week later, but the visit was made doubly tense by the fact that I was taking out his stepdaughter, who rang me two days before the interview to tell me she was late with her period and thought she might be pregnant. I then went into the meeting convinced I was going to lose my job and be forced into a shotgun wedding. Happily, after a well-earned reprimand, I was given a second chance and two days later, I got a telephone call from the girl saying that all was well. Phew!

I was to remain a total of six years at J Henry Schroder Wagg from 1960-1966. They were years, during which I learned a good deal. I even began to make myself useful by undertaking some investment research, which was an advance on doing valuations. Nowadays, valuations are produced in seconds on a computer updated with the previous night's closing prices. In the 1960s, however, it was considerably more laborious. Investment research required an ability to write and present a case and was more creative. I particularly remember an extensive study of the UK steel industry carried out for a director called the Honourable Alexander Hood. He wanted to know the value added per ingot tonne across all the dozen or so domestic British steel producers. It was a complicated exercise but I much enjoyed doing it. What use he could possibly have made of the information remains a mystery. I also wrote an analysis on mail order, which in the 1950s

My grandfather, Lindsay Bury

My father and mother; both died aged 33

Top Left My parents' wedding

Top Right My step parents' wedding

Sara and me. Mischief afoot

Eton leaving card; aged 17

Aunt Nancy on Jura with Harriet, 1984

Sara and Ken's happy day. They have just done 50 years!

Our big day. Never looked back!

Proud Dad: Young Frank

Hmmmmm. I'm not sure about that one

A.C.T.
Roger Foster with Bill Gates

The Apricot Computer.
Gates loved it!

Roger Foster, founder and CEO with LCNB, chairman and largest shareholder
– a 28 year relationship

Millichope Park before the bulldozers moved in

This picture shows why I had to live at Millichope on that site

The finished house with flotilla of swans on the lake

A Shaky Start and a Lot of Luck

was a fast-growing and increasingly popular method for store groups to reach their customers. This analysis attracted the attention of the directors, notably Michael Verey, head of J. Helbert Wagg and number two in the whole organisation, and some of the directors even acted on my recommendations.

Chapter Six
Political Adventure

It was about this time that I began to take an interest in politics. I became a member of the Bow Group and Coningsby Club, in which Nigel Lawson, David Howell, as well as Leon Brittan and other aspiring politicians from Cambridge were prominent, and it occurred to me that it would be good experience to fight an election for a hopeless Conservative seat.

Susie Aird, a girlfriend, was working at Conservative Central Office at the time and had a list of the sixty parliamentary constituencies in the West Midlands, all but four of which had already appointed candidates to fight the election. These were Birmingham Northfield, Stoke-on-Trent North, Stoke-on-Trent South and Stoke-on-Trent Central. It seemed to me that no harm would be done by having a go. There was no chance of a Conservative candidate winning any of these constituencies, but the experience of contesting a seat would be valuable so I had a word with Michael Verey, my boss at Schroders, who raised no objection. I then wrote to all four of the constituencies but only received a reply from one, Stoke-on-Trent North, who asked me to attend an interview; there would be a shortlist of three. All the Stoke seats were held by Labour with huge majorities, and there was no chance whatever of unseating the Labour Party in this part of the country

Fortified with this knowledge, I took a train from Euston to Stoke. I barely knew where it was, let alone any facts about the constituency that I aspired to represent. I tried to put this right by engaging in conversation with an elderly, grey-faced man who was sitting opposite me on the train and who turned out to come from Stoke. I learned from him the fact that the main industries in Stoke were potteries and coalmining. He was a dour, uncommunicative man but this was a start. On alighting from the train, I took a cab to a pub in Burslem, which doubled up as the Conservative offices for the Stoke North constituency. I shall never forget that cab ride; we passed rows and rows of semi-detached houses' interspersed with bottle-shaped brick buildings, which I later learned were the kilns for the potteries. There was also a substantial industrial structure, which turned out to be the Shelton Steel Works, long since closed.

Entering the pub mid-afternoon, there was nobody there except the barman who was polishing glasses and barely looked up. There seemed to be no sign of the aassociation offices so I asked him where they were and explained why I was there. He pointed to a narrow flight of stairs at the back of the bar. 'They're waiting for you up there.'

I climbed the stairs and the door opened into a room where six red-faced men were seated, facing a desk behind which there were two chairs, one of which was empty and clearly for me. The other was occupied by the chairman, Mr Thomas E Talbot who looked at his notes. 'This is Mr Bury,' he said. 'Would you like to say a few words, Mr Bury?'

I then proceeded to make a five minute speech which was embarrassingly bad, full of ums and errs, saying why

A Shaky Start and a Lot of Luck

I wanted to represent Stoke for the Conservative party at the coming election. I was received in complete silence. There was then one question from a man in the front row, with a particularly red face. 'What do you know about Stoke?'

I was prepared for this and relayed the information I had picked up in the train about pits and pots. This was again greeted again with complete silence and the chairman asked me to go and wait downstairs.

On descending the staircase, I saw the barman still hard at work polishing his glasses.

'Gosh I've blown that. I made a really bad speech,' I said.

The barman shook his head. 'Don't worry lad you'll be fine.'

'What about the other two candidates?' I asked. 'There's a shortlist of three.'

'Aye, but they've not turned up.'

At that point, the door opened upstairs and I was summoned back to the meeting.

Mr Talbot cleared his throat and announced: 'By a unanimous decision, you have been adopted as the prospective Conservative Party parliamentary candidate for Stoke-on-Trent North.'

Everybody rose to their feet and there followed what seemed to be a marathon bout of drinking. Mr Talbert's favourite, as I remember, was brandy and soda of which he drank a great many, and a few hours later, I collapsed onto a seat in the train back to London, feeling very drunk, and by no means sure that my entry into politics was a good idea.

Political Adventure

My adoption took place in very early 1966 and the general election was to be on March 31st. Harold Wilson, the new Labour leader, had defeated Alec Douglas Home by a very narrow margin in 1964. However, his majority was only four seats and two by-election defeats had reduced this to two, which was clearly not a working majority. Douglas Home had meanwhile given way as leader to Ted Heath. As I remember, the really decisive event which took place in 1965, was the Unilateral Declaration of Independence (UDI) by Ian Smith in what was then called Rhodesia. Harold Wilson went on the attack on television, and his mastery on the small screen was decisive in establishing his personality with the public. I remember at the party conference in Blackpool in February 1966, sitting in a room dominated by a large television set where Wilson was in full flow attacking Ian Smith. Robin Day, who was the precursor of Jeremy Paxman as chief political inquisitor on *Newsnight*, was watching, shaking his head in admiration. The 1966 election was very much a personal triumph for Wilson.

I had quite an eventful campaign starting with a visit down a coalmine, the Norton colliery in Burslem. The journey down in the lift seemed to go on forever and then there was an equally long horizontal tunnel taking us to the coalface. As we approached, the roof of the tunnel got lower, the walls narrower and the heat increased. Finally, we arrived at a brilliantly lit chamber where a revolving cutting head was stripping away large quantities of coal; it was very interesting and absorbing. I was then introduced to the head of the local branch of the National Union of

A Shaky Start and a Lot of Luck

Mineworkers, an enormous man with a helmet lamp on his head, covered in coal dust. He shook my hand and immediately asked me where I had been to school and I squeaked rather nervously, 'Eton College'.

There was no point lying! He just laughed.

I also went to the Conservative Party Conference in Blackpool where by far the best speaker was Ian McLeod. I remember him dissecting the top trio of the Labour Cabinet.

'George Brown......... where have all the flowers gone? Ian Stewart .... You will remember Ian Stewart? .... No........... you will not remember Ian Stewart.'

And so on. The timing was exquisite and it was terrific stuff.

I had two prominent politicians who came to speak for me in Stoke. One was Enoch Powell, who I thought was almost mad. None of the audience seemed to understand much of what he said, and I drove him back after the speech to his constituency in Wolverhampton. He said not a word during the whole of the drive, which I thought showed bad manners. The other speaker was Gerald Nabarro, with his handlebar moustache. He was altogether more effective, and charmed all the Tory ladies with a good rich diet of lower taxes, hanging and flogging, and other traditional Tory themes. It all went down very well particularly with the blue rinse ladies who quivered with delight at his jokes.

Meanwhile, I had to undertake a good deal of knocking on doors and canvassing. I was told that the most promising ward for the Conservatives in an altogether unpromising

Political Adventure

constituency, was Sneyd Green in Burslem, and it was there that I devoted most of my efforts, helped by quite a few friends, notably Hady Wakefield and Liz Bridgeman, who came to help with the canvassing. None of the locals came out with me. One problem was the constituents' dogs, mainly terriers, poodles and Alsatians. On my ringing the doorbell, the barking would start and often my Conservative Party message was barely audible. I once got quite a sharp nip on the ankle from a terrier. The terraces in Sneyd Green were interminable and frequently I had over three hundred houses to get round in an afternoon. Finally, the campaign reached a conclusion and polling day arrived; I received 11,000 votes, as opposed to my Labour opponent John Forester, a somewhat colourless schoolmaster, who got 27,000; my swing was considered quite creditable against a background of a Labour landslide, which left them with a parliamentary majority of 96 seats.

After the election, the local association were keen to readopt me but I'd had enough. Not only was the long drive to Stoke quite a chore, but in addition to constituency events, I was regularly requested to speak in other areas of the West Midlands, which involved preparation as well as further long drives. I found having to have an opinion about everything very tedious. I also have a short attention span, forget everybody's names, and most constituency events bored me. In any case, I needed to make some money and politics is certainly no good for that. When the matter was raised once again before the next election, my newly-married wife, Sarah, said I wasn't cut out for it and she was quite right. This then was the end of my political career and, although some years later when Jasper More, member of Parliament for Ludlow and descendant of the More family at Millichope, retired, I agonised long and hard about whether to put my name forward for what was, and still is, usually a safe Conservative seat. I decided against it and have never regretted it.

Chapter Seven
Marriage and Millichope

In 1968, on a skiing holiday in Klosters, Switzerland, I was looking around a bar when I spotted a girl with lovely, soulful eyes. I went straight across and introduced myself. She told me she was called Sarah; we started chatting and seemed to click right away.

This turned out to be the prelude to the most important event in my life. We found ourselves on the same plane flying back to England, and I discovered that she was 22 and in her final year at Trinity College Dublin. A courtship soon developed with her coming over to stay at the Old Laundry and me going over to visit her in Dublin. Our meetings were considerably complicated by the epidemic of foot and mouth disease in 1968, which directly affected our part of Shropshire, a quarantined area.

I soon went up to meet her family in Kirkcudbrightshire in South West Scotland. Her parents, Peter and Rhona Ingall, were welcoming and delightful and in fact her two brothers Simon and Micky were contemporaries from Eton, although I only knew them slightly at school. Corsock House, the family home, was a large Scottish-baronial type house, surrounded by a beautiful garden and majestic trees. I will never forget my first encounter with the family. I arrived in the evening after a long journey from London and was met by Peter Ingall, Sarah's father, who was busy stoking up a blazing fire in the large baronial hall. He was a larger-than-life character, who had had a successful career in the City and was immediately cheerful and welcoming. It must have been rather a tense moment for the family because I was a serious suitor for their young daughter aged only 22, and still at University. Moreover, I was a Catholic, which for Peter was a bit of a problem, my own family, Nancy and Jasper, lived at the exact opposite end of the UK on Horsey Island, and I had had, to say the least, a complicated and bewildering childhood. The whole family was there, Rhona, Sarah's mother, and Simon and Micky. They were immensely welcoming and I was immediately drawn to this stable, cheerful family.

I soon got to know some of the family idiosyncrasies. There was a universal obsession with the weather. Forecasting in South West Scotland must, at the best of times, be a difficult business, but the Ingalls were hard to please; if the predicted sunny interval was late in following the clearing shower, black gloom would descend on the whole household. I remember many years later at Simon's funeral, his son James recounted an episode where his father could be seen swearing at the television. 'You bitch, you promised us a high (ridge of high pressure) this weekend; just look out of the window!' The weather forecastress would have seen the usual Galloway afternoon rain drizzling down.

Meals also followed a reassuringly predictable sequence. Saturday lunch would be a magnificent joint of roast beef from Mr Grierson, the butcher from Castle Douglas, which reappeared cold on Sunday. On Monday, it was made up hot. By Tuesday, it was the turn of roast lamb, which saw the family through to the end of the week, although I think fish did sneak in on Friday. Peter Ingall and his son Micky were passionate rhododendron gardeners, and the family also farmed in a modest way with a small herd of Galloway cattle. Peter must have been a demanding employer. He would spot a few cows in the wrong field and exclaim loudly. 'What's Lindsay (the farm manager) doing keeping them on the house field? He ought to have moved them on by now.' He spent a lot of time prowling about and checking up on Lindsay. Taxation, or avoiding paying it, was another keen interest, particularly of Peter's. There was a memorable episode when we were out on a modest family grouse shoot at Gatehouse of Fleet. We'd had a lovely day walking the beautiful moor without seeing too many grouse and Peter was the end gun on the last drive of the day. A handsome covey was flushed and flew directly over him, only to find him with his nose buried in Butterworth's Taxation Guide. Our hopes of a good bag, or indeed, a bag at all, were thereby dashed, but to huge amusement. It was a wonderful household with which I fell in love, as well as with Sarah.

Sarah and I got engaged during the summer holidays of the same year, after a whirlwind courtship, and were married in September 1968. We have now been married very nearly fifty years. She has been the most wonderful life's companion, as well as a constant source of fun. She has been an unfailing support and fount of advice in all my ventures; her judgement has always been shrewd and to the point. She has also led a very full and rewarding life in doing unpaid voluntary work, as well as serving on the District Council as chairman of Planning and as chairman of Ludlow College and, more recently, as chairman of the Shropshire Branch of the CPRE. She has, too, been a

Marriage and Millichope

wonderful mother to our two children Frank and Harriet and, in recent years, granny to our seven grandchildren. My marriage was the beginning of the most settled and happy time of my life. From now on she will appear constantly in this narrative.

The first and most pressing decision she helped me to make was to rebuild Millichope, which by that time had been empty for seven years and was deteriorating badly. I had met an architect, Nicholas Johnston, who was the son-in-law of Christopher Chancellor, the then chairman of Bowaters. Christopher often came to Millichope as the shooting guest of Malcolm Graham, the local newspaper tycoon in Wolverhampton, and a member of the Millichope shooting syndicate. He introduced me to Nicky as 'a very talented boy'.

Although Nicholas had made his reputation in converting existing structures and old houses he initially suggested it might be possible to build a new house on the site of Millichope, demolishing the existing house. We examined this possibility thoroughly. Since I had been hearing so many depressing appraisals of the existing house, which was by now very damp, having been without inhabitants for seven years, and would need re-roofing, as well as extensive structural alteration, the idea of starting again with a modern house had some attraction, particularly as Millichope had far more space than was needed for a home for a young couple.

However, one insurmountable problem was the size of the site and the levels. Millichope sits on a terrace cut into a steep slope, which runs down to a three-acre lake in front of the house, and from behind rises up to the top of the Wenlock Edge. The width of the balustrade at the front of the terrace is about a hundred yards. The important views of the house were below, from across the lake and from the terraced garden to the southwest. Any modern house would have to be tall enough to adequately occupy the site, standing up well above the terrace, while not being sited so far forward on the terrace as to look puny and insubstantial from the side. Although the house I inherited was really too big for the site, any modern house providing the conventional number of reception rooms and bedrooms would be too small to adequately fill it. Money, of course, was a factor and demolition and rebuilding would be dauntingly expensive. I was at my wits' end. As sometimes happens, however, my mind was made up by a complete stranger. I went to see an old girlfriend who had an Italian cousin staying. He was a layabout and a bit of a playboy and he took one look at the photograph of the facade and portico of Millichope that I showed him.

'You cannot possibly pull down this 'ouse; it ees magnificent,' he declared. 'You must keep eet and live there.'

I reflected for a while and then realised that he was absolutely right. Whatever the complications and cost, keeping the house would mean that at least we would have the same beautiful structure, which had stood for one hundred and thirty years. Sarah was all for it and the decision was made; we were going to convert the existing house and make it habitable. That was what we were going to do. Sarah had come into this halfway through the decision-making process and, having herself been brought

Marriage and Millichope

up in a large house, was unfazed by the challenge of converting Millichope. We were not helped, however, by the Historic Buildings Council, whose representative, a man called Slater, showed up with a Brownie camera and took pictures of the columns of the portico. 'You can build whatever you like,' he said, 'but don't remove the pillars.'

This advice was ignored, and we started Nicky on the challenge of designing a conversion. Once the decision was made, it didn't take long to settle on the details and we finally took the plunge, having retained a quantity surveyor and a remarkable firm of builders from Ludlow, Treasure & Sons. The go-ahead button was finally pressed.

It is difficult to describe the conversion that we finally undertook but, essentially, we decided to dispense with all the ground floor rooms, including the main front entrance, by filling in the lower portico entrance, which led up from a large gravel turning circle at the front of the house. The trouble with the front entrance from below, was that it led up into the middle of the main hall. This not only made the house much more difficult to heat but it also ruined the proportions of the hall, which is the most dramatic and impressive room in the house, taking up almost half of the space in the main building. In addition, we decided to fill in the lower courtyard to the north side of the house, creating a courtyard on the first floor, accessible to arriving cars, and build a new main entrance to the north on this level. A wing linking the main house with an adjacent servants' house was pulled down, and the lawn from the lake was embanked right up to the main retaining wall, under the portico. It was a very big job involving a great deal of earth moving. Many of the main rooms were altered with additional interior walls, particularly on the first floor and we re-sited several fireplaces. The estimate for the whole job was £100,000, in 1970, a lot of money and the time to complete was one year. Both these targets were achieved. We had monthly site meetings with the builders and architects, but Sarah and I were very inexperienced and we made few alterations to the original plan. I have to say that in the forty-two years Sarah and I lived at Millichope, the builders hardly ever had to come back. They did an amazing job.

I had received a grant from the Historic Buildings Council of £15,000 and, about halfway through the contract, when the stock market was falling sharply, I was concerned whether or not I would be able to afford to complete the contract. However, the market eventually recovered and my fortunes, aided by an investment in Lesney Products (which I'll go into later), improved dramatically. During the downturn, I had been removing various items from the specification which came under the heading 'desirable but not essential', but, when the market rallied, I put them all back in again and also decided to repay the HBC grant. There are always strings attached to public money and in this case it entailed providing access to the public to go round the house. I didn't much relish this, considering it an intrusion upon our privacy and rather a chore. Having repaid the grant I received a very courteous reply congratulating me on my 'honourable gesture' in repaying it. There was nothing very honourable about it. I simply didn't want the public trailing about the house.

Marriage and Millichope

Nicky Johnston also introduced Sarah and me to David Mlinaric, then an up-and-coming interior decorator, whose work had hitherto been mainly in restaurants, nightclubs and houses for various London-based clients. Millichope was to be his first major country house commission, and his decoration of all the principal reception rooms aroused widespread admiration. Nicky's conversion also received approval except from a Marc Girouard, who wrote a stroppy letter to the *Country Life* magazine, complaining about 'Mr Johnston's earthworks'.

We had to have a decorator because the great size of the rooms at Millichope, particularly the hall, meant that mistakes were likely to be very expensive. Even though I have now passed the house over to my son, Frank, none of the main rooms have needed redecorating after nearly fifty years, with the exception of the dining room which has been restored to its original proportions. David charged us £400 per room, and also found us some badly-needed furniture and chose the curtains. He has now just retired, having risen to the height of his profession with an international reputation.

Happily, Millichope was very well built. Not only the stonework, sourced from Grinshill quarry just north of Shrewsbury, but also the mahogany doors, oak sash windows and floors were built to last and, notwithstanding the requirement to re-roof, the whole house, the excellence of the original structure has stood us in good stead.

Chapter Eight
Singer & Friedlander

After I'd decided not to pursue a career in politics, I was wondering what to do next. I could have gone back to Schroders but didn't find the prospect very appealing and, before long, I was contacted by Michael Stoddart, a friend from Shropshire who was setting up an office in Birmingham for Singer & Friedlander, the City merchant bank for which he worked. Michael had a vision of bringing merchant banking to the provinces, particularly with a thrust towards corporate finance. Singer & Friedlander was a small bank founded and run by two Austrian Jewish brothers, Hans and Francis Hock, who had emigrated to London in the 1930s, along with others like Walter Salomon and Sigmund Warburg. Their main business was lending money to clients, for the purchase of gilt edged securities registered in the bank's name for the purpose of stripping out the dividends. They had also ventured, to a limited extent, into the world of mortgage lending, using extremely conservative ratios of valuation. Michael managed to persuade them that Singer and Friedlander could be a little more venturesome and open up in the provinces, earning good fees for corporate finance advisory work such as flotation, mergers and acquisitions, all of which offered handsome fees, without putting S&F's balance sheet at risk. There was also a feeling that anything that happened north of Watford would not make much impact on the bank's reputation, and so it was a case of a suck it and see. The first office was established in Leeds and Michael,

Singer & Friedlander

together with Brian Buckley, soon established a profitable business there. After two or three years, Michael had set about opening up in the much larger city of Birmingham.

Singer and Friedlander opened their offices in the Hagley Road, situated next door to the Plough and Harrow Hotel, which at the time had one of the better restaurants in the city. The first employees were Michael Mander and Charles Blunt, who had good connections in Wolverhampton and Derbyshire, but brought no particular technical expertise. Shortly afterwards, Sir Timothy Harford joined; this was something of a coup, since he had been for a number of years working for our most established competitor, Birmingham Industrial Trust (BIT). Tim had a thorough knowledge of corporate finance, having already led several transactions for them. I joined at about the same time, aged 28, with a good training in investment management from my six years at Schroder Wagg. Tim and I also had our own contacts in the Midlands. All five of us sat in the same room, and the atmosphere was extremely stimulating and great fun. Over the seven years I was there, I learned a great deal.

The competition in Birmingham was not strong. After BIT had lost Tim, they seemed to disappear from the scene and I cannot recall any significant deals that they did after his departure. There was also a long-established, industrial holding group called Neville Securities, owned and run by the Dawes family. Their real days of glory were back in the fifties, when they were the market leader and floated many small companies in Birmingham. By the time we appeared, however, the management had passed to the son, Howard

A Shaky Start and a Lot of Luck

Dawes, whose interests lay mainly in architecture. He was quite content for Neville to live on its assets, and the business was neglected.

Michael rapidly established a dominant position. He was a charismatic presence; cheerful, optimistic and highly energetic, he loved deals and spoke the same language as our entrepreneurial clients, who felt he was an exception to the received image of pompous city gentlemen who patronised and lectured their clients. Instead of pointing out the difficulties and drawbacks of the various deals they wanted to do, Michael was supportive, always giving the impression that he really wanted their business and that it was fun dealing with S&F. For a seven year period, from 1966-73, we enjoyed a string of successes, floating about twenty companies, and establishing a highly profitable operation that greatly increased the reputation and profitability of Singer & Friedlander.

An important step was winning the support of the professional firms in the city, notably the lawyers, accountants and stockbrokers. This was not entirely straightforward, because the larger brokers were quite capable of handling flotations on their own. In fact, adding the services of an issuing house such as S&F usually meant the client had to pay more in fees. Michael's skill lay in persuading the clients that it was worth paying more to get the on-the-spot advice that came from dealing with a locally based issuing house, such as S&F, rather than a remote London stockbroker or, indeed, a local Birmingham firm with limited capability and inferior placing power. Before long, we obtained the support of the professional firms in the city, who came to value our business and were wary of competing directly with us. Apart from routine merger and acquisition work, we carried out a succession of successful flotations and worked with a handful of top firms; L. Messel was our top broker, Peter Spicer being the main partner concerned. Richard Westmacott, of C. Hoare and Co, was another important broker for us. We worked with some outstanding personalities among the Birmingham professional firms. The solicitors, Christopher Harmer at Pinsents and Theo Christophers at Ryland Martineau, were top class lawyers, while John Adcock, senior partner at Peat Marwick (later KPMG), was probably the most powerful figure in the partnership outside London. They became firm allies and we all benefited from sending each other business.

Over a six-year period, the following flotations were carried out by the Birmingham office of Singer & Friedlander:

- The Greaves Organisation - house builders; CEO Ted Wheatley
- David Charles - house builders; CEO Robin Buckingham
- Allied Carpets - carpet retailers; CEO Harold Plotnek
- Brierleys Supermarkets - discount retailers
- Turner Manufacturing - manufacturer of truck axels and gear boxes; CEOs Chris & Roy Dumbell.
- York Trailer - manufacturer of trailers; CEO Fred Davis

A Shaky Start and a Lot of Luck

- Dom Holdings - distributor of fastenings; CEO Douglas MacIntyre
- Sealed Motor Construction - pump manufacturer; CEO Philip Pensabene
- Prew Smith Knitwear - hosiery manufacturer; CEO Harry Prew Smith
- Contour Hosiery - lingerie manufacturer
- Ashworth & Stewart – builders; CEO Arthur Jordan
- Lennons Supermarkets - supermarkets in Lancashire; CEO Terence Lennon
- Kwik Save Discount - supermarkets; CEO Albert Gubay

This list is not complete but it gives a flavour of the kind of companies that we served. The founders and bosses of these firms were, in most cases, remarkable characters. Plotnek was a good example. He had two companies - Allied Carpets and Greaves Organisation. Allied Carpets were a discount retailer of carpets, while Greaves were a house builder, one of whose specialities was buying up the handsome Victorian houses with large gardens that proliferated in Edgbaston, and covering the gardens with bungalows. Not great to look at, but very profitable. I got to know him well and I used to attend Birmingham Jewish gatherings on a Sunday night as his guest. We floated his company at 168p, and before long the shares had risen to over 300p. Then the stock market slumped and Allied Carpets' shares fell to 18p. I remember sitting in his office, watching him fume about the share price. He waved his latest months accounts at me. 'Look at last month's figures! We're making good money and we have plenty of cash. What do these buggers know that I don't?'

The shares soon rose again, to 200p, Plotnek having bought several million at 20p. I joined in the fun and bought a few myself.

Albert Gubay of Kwik Save Discount was a particularly tough customer. He personally used to lay the foundations of his own supermarkets in North Wales. In fact, when we first visited him, he was wearing a string vest and clutching a pickaxe, and Michael thought he was one of the builders. He had established a formidably effective business model for building a chain of discount supermarkets, based on carrying a limited line of basic household staples, and a highly effective proprietary computer system. An important line was toilet paper. 'Half a roll per hole per week,' was the company motto. He had had a row with Bowaters, his main supplier of lavatory paper. Kimberley Clark, a rival supplier, were desperate to get into Kwik Save and they offered Gubay a cheaper paper than Bowaters, who duly responded by cutting their own price. The stakes were high; it was said that a paper making machine at Bowaters depended on this account. After several offers and counter offers, Kimberley Clark suggested to Gubay that Bowaters' roll contained fewer sheets than theirs. Gubay reacted strongly to this, and invited both salesmen to present themselves with their rolls, and to unroll them across the boardroom carpet for the sheets to be counted. Kimberley Clark proved to be right; Bowaters roll did, indeed, contain fewer sheets, and fewer than specified. Bowaters duly lost the contract and Gubay demanded a refund for all the missing sheets that he had paid for over the previous years!

Kwik Save's flotation was a huge success. Unfortunately, soon after the flotation, Gubay left the business and decamped to New Zealand, after selling most of his shares, in contravention of his agreement with us, and a few years later Kwik Save was sold. It had done phenomenally well and had the potential to become a very large business as Aldi and Lidl, with an almost identical business model, have proved today!

Terence Lennon was another larger-than-life character. He had a strong local presence in central Lancashire, where Lennons had a cluster of supermarkets, but his great weakness was champagne, particularly Dom Perignon, of which he drank prodigious amounts. Even a morning meeting would find him in the boardroom, face flushed, with a bottle half-consumed, which made him somewhat difficult to deal with and the company and its advisors relied heavily on the long-suffering finance director, John Bolton to keep the ship afloat. I don't remember that the chairman's love of Dom Perignon featured in the prospectus when we floated the company.

My own role in the management team was twofold. In the first instance, I set up the investment management activity in the Birmingham office. As the principal shareholders in the various companies floated their companies, they found themselves suddenly in possession of sizeable amounts of cash for investment. Dealing with these people was not easy, for they were very tough and understandably suspicious of handing over the management of their money on a discretionary basis. It was much easier dealing with their wives and their children's trustees, but my business grew very well nonetheless.

My second job was to go out to meet many of the large number of small companies listed on the Midland Stock Exchange, with a view to interesting them in some form of corporate activity, thereby becoming clients of Singers. Most of these companies had a listing in name only; minimal turnover took place in their shares, yet they had to put out statements to the exchange, and comply with all the regulatory requirements. Being quoted, so far as I could see, brought them no benefit whatever. However, they were always pleased to see prospective investors who took an interest in their companies; in those days, insider dealing did not carry the severe penalties which obtain today. I remember one man, Bill Sidaway, boss of Ductile Steels in Wednesfield, who said five minutes after I entered his office, 'Well you buggers are only interested in the figures so have a look at this and then we'll go and have lunch,' whereupon he would chuck over the cumulative sales and profit figures from the last board meeting. After lunch, having consumed a number of stiff gin and tonics, we were led off to the Number 1 Planetary Mill, which involved slabs of molten steel being passed through a series of rollers which reduced it from two inches thick to one half inch. I found this very satisfying to watch and this was typical of many visits, drop forging being particularly noisy, and it was sometimes impossible to hear what was being said. Often, they just wanted a good gossip; it was particularly informative hearing what they said about their competitors.

Another memorable visit was to Typhoo Teas in Bordesley, near New Street Station in Birmingham. The boss there was a legendary figure called Harry Kelly, whose balance sheet showed a hoard of £25 million in cash, which was no mean sum in the 1960s. Michael and I entered his office and were taken aback to see a room devoid of all furniture except a desk, with him sitting behind it, linoleum rather than carpet on the floor, and lighting consisting of one bulb without a shade, hanging from the ceiling over his desk. Control of costs was the big theme at Typhoo! The only thing they spent real money on was advertising, and he certainly wasn't interested in any of the services we had to offer. I noted with astonishment the enormous price paid by Cadbury Schweppes for the company when he sold out a few years later.

One particularly important visit I made was to a lock manufacturing company, Lowe and Fletcher. The business was situated in Willenhall, near Wolverhampton and the chairman, Philip Trevor Jones, I knew socially. Philip suggested that I should join a works outing with his engineers to visit a company in east London, called Lesney Products, to whom Lowe and Fletcher were a large supplier of die castings. Lesney was of course the firm that made 'Matchbox' model cars. We set off in a charabanc, arriving in due course at an enormous factory in Lee Conservancy Road, Hackney, in East London. I was amazed at the volume of these model cars being churned out. After an extremely bullish presentation, I asked the works manager what were his greatest problems, and the reply was: production; not being able build enough to meet demand. 80% of turnover was exported and the world couldn't get enough of the little toy cars. However, he did tell me that they had recently installed some new die casting machines that could produce four castings in a cycle, as opposed to two, and that these were making good inroads into the backlog of demand. They had only been installed for a couple of months. I then did some sums looking back over the company's recent profit and loss account, and reckoned that the stock market was unaware of the big lift in output enabled by the new machines. I bought a lot of shares. Sure enough, when the figures came out, the market was completely wrong-footed by the very large jump in profit, and the shares soared. This took place in the middle of the Millichope building contract and enabled me to restore and even increase many of the projects that I'd previously had to scratch. After that Millichope became known as *Matchbox Hall.*

 I visited a large number of companies over the years I was with Singer and Friedlander, and learned a great deal about the industries of Birmingham and the Black Country. I also developed a great respect for the Birmingham entrepreneurs. Tough and ruthless in most cases, they were nonetheless the backbone of the Midlands economy; they worked hard, took big risks, gave employment to a lot of people, and presumably paid their taxes. They were also great fun to be with, and my years at S&F were some of the most enjoyable of my business career. It makes me sad to have witnessed the huge decline in manufacturing industry in the West Midlands. The trouble is that many of the smaller engineering companies were metal bashers, adding little value and, with globalisation, they could not compete with low-cost producers in India and the Far East. All the steel works closed, and many of the large motor components and general engineering companies were hit very hard. It is only now, twenty-five years later, that the dependence on manufacturing has been reduced and the local economy is more broadly based. Currently, an upswing is taking place and the West Midlands is recovering from a long period of under-performance relative to the rest of the UK economy. I have recently in my retirement returned to Birmingham, but as a property investor and I am very heartened by the transformation of the city that is now taking place.

Shortly before I left Singer and Friedlander, an entertaining episode took place. I was approached by Henry Hely-Hutchinson, who was the UK manager of IOS (Investors Overseas Services), with a view to becoming one of their investment managers. IOS was an extraordinary phenomenon which took place in the mid-70s. It was an offshore US company, set up to manage the savings of American servicemen stationed primarily in Germany. These amounted to very large sums, and the bosses of IOS were a bunch of colourful gangsters, chief among whom were Bernie Cornfeld, the CEO and founder, and Ed Cowitt, the investment chief, who placed vast amounts of investors' money in Arctic land which, before long, had to be totally written off. Their investment management policy in Britain was to spread the management of the money through a number of managers, each of whom would compete with each other on performance on a monthly basis.

It was an asinine system, but there was nothing to be lost and I signed a contract and started out with an allocation of $100,000. The best performing manager was given additional sums to manage, which were withdrawn from the least successful manager. It was quite obvious to me at the time that the UK was in a severe bear market. I therefore did nothing and, the following month, the sum at my disposal rose to $200,000. This went on for months, because my competitors were fully invested and, before long, I was managing millions of dollars and the management fee entitlement was considerable. I continued to do nothing and, in fact throughout my eighteen months as manager, I do not remember buying a single share; but the computer continued to allocate me more cash since I was not losing money and doing better than my rivals. The contract was in my name and when I made the decision to leave Singer & Friedlander and set up Dunbar, I vaguely wondered who was entitled to the IOS contract. However, I didn't want to have a row with Singers and I had only obtained the contract due to my position as manager there, so I did nothing. I did wonder afterwards, whether my successor who took on the contract continued with my successful policy of total inertia.

Chapter Nine
Home Life

While I was commuting into Singer & Friedlanders' office in Birmingham during the first years of our marriage, Nicky Johnston and Treasures were completing the contract to build Millichope and eventually in 1970 we moved in. I shall never forget the first night we spent there. The kitchen, where we ate most meals, faced out into the hill at the back of the house, and I remember looking up the bank behind the house from my chair in the kitchen at the evening light streaming through the enormous lime trees on the bank, and thinking how wonderful it was and what a dramatic place to have moved into. From every room in the house, the view was commanding and beautiful, and I felt enormous satisfaction that Sarah and I had finally pulled it off and moved in without going bankrupt in the process. We had virtually no furniture; my grandfather, after the war, had reached the understandable conclusion that subsequent generations would not be able to afford to live in a house such as Millichope, and most of the furniture had been sold, although various paintings had been loaned to the Ludlow District Council, which we were eventually able to recover. Of the five major reception rooms on the ground floor, three were completely unfurnished: the hall, the drawing room and the music room.

We lived for the first two years entirely in the kitchen and the library. The library, the nearest thing we had to a cosy room, had its original bookcases and pelmets and a substantial number of books, mostly leather-bound, although many of them were in bad condition, resulting from years of storage in a damp cellar. In the evenings, we would cross diagonally over the hall from the kitchen and go and sit there, where we would light a good fire and watch television. Upstairs, the views were even more amazing than from the ground floor, although we furnished the bedrooms fairly conventionally and cheaply. A lot of friends came to stay, and nobody minded that the house seemed somewhat spartan and under-furnished. Our two children, Frank and Harriet were born and we had a happy start to our life at Millichope. At roughly the same time, my sister Sara got married to a Londoner called Kenneth Moore. He was a print broker, specialising in placing contracts for photographic envelopes. It was of vital concern who my sister married, after all we had been through together, and it is grand to relate that they have had a wonderfully happy marriage with three children and nine grandchildren. They have lived in London and in Shropshire, in my grandfather's old house, Munslow Cottage, and they have just celebrated their fiftieth wedding anniversary.

 Once we were more or less settled in the house, we set about restoring the garden. This was always going to be a mammoth task, since it comprised eleven acres, with some formal borders and lawns on the upper terraces next to the house, with a three-acre lawn leading down to the lake at a lower level. The job of felling, clearing and burning started even before I was married, and many of my friends still remember weekends of toil in the Millichope gardens.

A Shaky Start and a Lot of Luck

However, when Sarah appeared on the scene she took charge. She knew a fair amount about big gardens, having been brought up at Corsock, now one of the best rhododendron gardens in Scotland. The business of clearing was accelerated, and about sixty trees were felled within about two years. New borders were established and plantings undertaken; my aunt Penelope Nix had helped to a limited extent, but when Sarah appeared on the scene she gave way to the new management. Sarah was to be in charge of the garden for the next 42 years while we lived there, and Millichope is now ranked as a garden of national importance, and is a joy to walk round. All this she has done with the help of one full-time gardener and an assistant.

During this period, I also took over responsibility for running Millichope Estate. I was very short of money, following the purchase of my sister's half of the estate in March 1968, and paying for the conversion of the house in 1970, even though my fortunes were beginning to improve from my activities in Birmingham. I was also personally guaranteeing substantial borrowings by a company, ACT, in which I had taken a large holding, and before long, subscribing capital for Dunbar, two ventures which I'll go into in detail later. Suffice it to say that both of these businesses were highly risky; I could easily have got into serious trouble and might have had to sell much of the estate, which I had only recently bought, had they gone wrong. Indeed, I wasn't able personally to complete the purchase of my sister Sara's half of the estate; I needed help from my father-in-law Peter Ingall to purchase one of the farms, Broadstone. He had considerable misgivings at first, but was finally persuaded to allocate some funds from a trust which he had set up for Sarah, but I was still obliged to leave one of the farms, Munslow Farm, in my sister's hands because I hadn't enough cash to buy it from her. Because I was working full-time in Birmingham, I retained the services of a land agency firm, Godfrey Payton, based in Warwickshire, where the partner concerned, Henry Feilding, had been a nephew of my step-grandmother, Gertrude. Like my stepfather Hilary Lewis, he was an army officer returning from the war who had qualified as a land agent. The farms were all let and the woods were by and large immature, so there wasn't a great deal to do. To relieve my cash problems, I sold some cottages, which I later came to regret but the need for cash was urgent, particularly in view of the requirement to furnish Millichope and, in due course, pay school fees. So, for the next twenty years the estate basically ticked over and no great decisions were required. I drew no money out because I was just about able to live on my salary from Singer & Friedlander, and only routine cottage repairs and improvements were done.

As a landlord, I can't say I was particularly good or bad but, many years later, I received a message from the land agent that a little old lady, Mrs Powell Bevan, who had occupied a cottage and smallholding for a great many years, had said she would 'Very much like to meet Mr Bury because he had been such a wonderful landlord.' Somewhat surprised, I duly went round and was shocked to see the old thing huddled in a chair in a freezing living room, with an electric fire blowing hot air up her skirt. We sat close together and held hands and, in fact, it was so cold that I tried to manoeuvre my trouser leg across to share in the warm draught. We had a lovely chat, and this was the first of several visits I made before she died. I felt thoroughly ashamed that the house wasn't warmer, and we did install a good modern stove. The only reason she could possibly think I was a good landlord was that the rent was so low!

One crisis soon occurred, which potentially could have cost me a lot of money. The largest farm on the estate, situated halfway up the Wenlock Edge, was called Upper Millichope Farm, and when the old tenant Jack Edwards died, I decided for some reason not to re-let the farm to his sons, and to take it in hand. My neighbour on an adjacent farm, Upper Stanway, was a Major Guy Radcliffe. I knew him a bit socially, and the idea dawned that it might be a good idea to go into partnership with him. This would give me more flexibility and possibly bring in more income than renewing the Edwards' tenancy, and I would avoid tying up the farm for another generation. His son, Julian Radcliffe, told me what a successful chap he was and when I ran the idea past the Major, he jumped at it. Without bothering with any check-ups or due diligence, we established our partnership.

Initially, things seemed to go quite well although there was no profit, which seemed a bit surprising. The Major, who spoke with a patrician drawl, seemed to be primarily interested in the general tidiness of the farm. 'This is a rural slum!' was one of his favourite expressions. He would stride about my farm in his army jodhpurs, which were his normal farming clothes, pointing out rural slums everywhere. Communications were an obsession, presumably reflecting his army background; the siting of gates into fields and the tracks between them interested him intensely. One thing which was never mentioned was money, or profit and loss, which was for me rather more interesting. He had a beautiful herd of pure Hereford cattle in which he took great pride. I was at that stage unaware that having a single-suckler pedigree beef herd was an impossible way to make a profit. However, he was a genial chap, I was busy in Birmingham and I didn't take too much interest in the venture. When in due course he said he wanted to buy Blackwood Farm, a small holding between his land and mine, and asked if he could pay for it through the partnership account, I agreed, not having any idea what a risky and stupid step this was. The Major's bank at the time was C.Hoare & Co in Fleet Street, and he was always telling me about his excellent relationship with Quentin Hoare, one of the partners.

Sure enough, one day the Major rang to inform me that the bank were not prepared to advance him funds to complete his purchase of Blackwood Farm, which would therefore have to remain on the partnership account. Hoares were understandably unwilling to countenance a transfer, which would increase their risk exposure to Major Radcliffe. At this point, alarm bells belatedly began ringing in my mind and I went off to see my local manager at Lloyds Bank, Bill Woods. He very quickly brought home to me that I was in big trouble, and was shouldering all financial risk of the partnership, together, indeed, with the personal finances of Major Radcliffe. I was thoroughly alarmed, because I was financially overextended on so many other fronts. I then remonstrated with Hoares saying that the purchase of Blackwood Farm was nothing to do with me and it should not have been put through the partnership account in the first place. At which point any other bank would have said, 'Too bad. You signed. You are liable.' Hoares, however, acknowledged that the charge was not appropriate and they made Guy sell Blackwood Farm. Finally this was done and my loan was repaid in full. I was very lucky, having suffered quite a few sleepless nights over the episode, and I learned a valuable lesson. I have never forgotten how leniently I was treated by Hoares, and I am pleased to say that I am now once again a substantial customer of the bank.

Chapter Ten
Dunbar

In 1973 Michael Stoddart, my boss for the past seven years, announced that he was to leave Singer and Friedlander to take up a position as managing director of Electra Investment Trust. By then, Singer and Friedlander had been taken over by insurance giant, C T Bowring. I was surprised and rather dismayed by the news. I didn't think the Birmingham office would prosper without Mike. Tim Harford, although an excellent transactor of business, was not a promoter and salesman and I came to the conclusion that Singers' halcyon days were probably over and although the managing director's job had by then been taken over by Tony Solomons, whom I much admired, with Mike still a main board director, I felt it was time to move on.

It wasn't going to be easy to find something suitable if I remained in Birmingham which, despite the long and boring forty mile commute to and from Millichope, was what I wanted to do. After several abortive attempts at setting up a new venture, I became aware that my cousin David Backhouse was attempting to buy control of a small secondary bank called Dunbar. This seemed a promising idea, because Dunbar was already established with the relevant money-lending licences, and had an established business with depositors and loan customers, and a small office in Pall Mall in the West End of London. The bank had been set up in 1969 by three county figures from the south west of Scotland, David Hope Dunbar and two others; the name Dunbar which they had adopted, seemed Scottish and respectable and they set up in business. Before long, however, they were bought out by a syndicate of investors from Glasgow, including notably Sir Iain Stewart, of Fairfield Shipyard fame, and the actor Sean Connery. The Glaswegians supplied some capital but they had nobody who knew anything about banking. David Backhouse came from Wallace Brothers Sassoon Bank with a good banking pedigree, and he was in the process of negotiating a deal whereby he would subscribe some capital and become chief executive. I suggested to David that I could bring some investment clients and also inject some capital, but I wished to continue to operate from Birmingham. It seemed a good idea, because the cash balances of the investment clients together with my own investment would bring some liquidity and stability and provide some useful fee income to improve the profits. Birmingham was also a much cheaper place from which to operate than the West End of London.

So I subscribed £120,000 of new capital and joined the board. This was in November 1973. We were then almost immediately hit by a huge disaster in the shape of the fringe bank crisis of 1973. The 1960s had seen a proliferation of strange money lending organisations (such as Dunbar!) and in the autumn of 1973 a crisis struck the banks, provoked by the insolvency of London and County Securities in November, to be followed shortly after by that of First National Finance and United Dominions Trust. The Bank of England hastily established 'the Lifeboat', which bailed out about 30 of the smaller banks and intervened to assist a further 30, an exercise that cost the UK taxpayer an estimated £100 million. While all these institutions were left able to pay out their depositors, fear gripped the market, and even the National Westminster Bank found it necessary to issue a reassuring statement about its solvency. The wholesale money markets dried up, deposits were recalled and re-deposited with the handful of clearing banks still regarded as safe. It was against this background that I invested my £120,000; I thought for a while that I might be paying it straight to the receiver!

Dunbar could well have succumbed very quickly. Like everyone else, we relied on money market funds and we certainly had our fair share of non-performing loans. The loss of a handful of key depositors could have caused a run on the bank within hours. I vividly remember some of the dubious characters to whom the bank had lent money. There was an American called Brauch, who had borrowed about £150,000 from us and bought a building in St Peter's Port, Guernsey. He owed money all over the place and the prospects of selling the Guernsey building were not good. He attended meetings in a dirty raincoat, while consuming peanuts out of a bag. It took us years to recover our loans from him. Another was an art dealer called Von Kassel; our loan was secured against modern works of art which were highly speculative and mostly unsaleable. Apparently, there was one of a nude woman with a lobster on top of her backside, although I never set eyes on this. I forget how much that went for! Some of Dunbar's deposits were withdrawn, but David did a fantastic job in going round the City, visiting our creditors and reassuring them that we were solvent and had a robust business plan. By the skin of our teeth, we survived. Enough of the larger depositors remained loyal and, over a period of years, we slowly managed to recover most of the loans, while gradually reserving for the ones which we would never get back. The investment business which I introduced was certainly helpful. Regulation in those days, both of banks and investment management houses, was much less onerous than today. Even now I shudder to think what would have happened to my investment customers' deposits, had we gone bust. Whether they would have been shielded from the bank's creditors, I very much doubt. However, once again I was lucky and we survived.

Working at Dunbar was very congenial. I got on well with my cousin David, who did a good job looking after the bank in London, which was where most of the risk lay. We had an excellent small office at 53 Pall Mall, just off St James's Square, with a lunchroom where Sir Iain Stewart, one of our Glasgow directors, used to bring along some very entertaining and useful lunch guests. I remember several of them. Albert Finney the actor, John Stonehouse the disappearing Labour politician, Clive Jenkins the smarmy Welsh leader of one of the white-collar unions, also some top businessmen and potential allies such as Dennis Martin Jenkins of the Ellerman Line. We also acquired a chairman, Michael Allsopp, in 1979 from Allen Harvey and Ross, the discount house.

I vividly remember one episode in St James's Square, just behind our Pall Mall office, which had nothing to do with banking. A big commotion took place in 1984 in the square, a few hundred yards from my office, caused by a member of the Libyan Embassy staff, in response to a demonstration taking place in the square outside the embassy, shooting dead a young policewoman, Yvonne Fletcher. Leon Brittan, my friend from Cambridge, had by then become Home Secretary and was in charge of the government's response to this murder but, unbelievably, due presumably to diplomatic immunity, the wretched man was spirited out of the country and no charges could be brought. It seems incredible that you can murder somebody in another country and escape prosecution due to diplomatic immunity; more recently the Russians seem to have cottoned onto the idea. I certainly hope there is still an open file on this episode, which continues to haunt me every time I walk across St James's Square and see a memorial to Yvonne, which always is bedecked with flowers.

Back in Birmingham, I had acquired premises in Frederick Road, not far from the Singer and Friedlander offices, but the other side of the Five Ways interchange. I recruited three or four staff and set up the structure for running an investment department. My secretary, Linda Collins, came with me from Singers and we had a low-cost profitable operation. I also recruited a crucially important addition to the investment department, although he worked from the London office. This was my brother-in-law, Micky Ingall. Micky came from Scrimgeours, the stockbrokers, and he was an invaluable addition to our small team, joining the Dunbar board in 1978. Apart from being a good investor and bringing in clients, he was an exceptionally able man, and some years later when Dunbar was eventually sold, Micky went on to found Rathbones, which he built into one of the largest and best regarded fund management houses in the City. In 1980, we made a second important recruit to the investment side, Jonathan Ruffer. He had previously been a barrister and had, like myself, done a spell at Schroders. He also developed into a shrewd and perceptive investor and. after the sale of Dunbar and a period working with Micky at Rathbones, he went on to establish his own investment management company, Ruffer, and has made a major fortune. I am proud that the founders of Rathbones and Ruffer spent some of their formative years working at Dunbar!

However, there were more traumatic events in store for us. The fringe bank crisis was followed by the 1973-74 stock market crash, one of the worst downturns in modern history. The Dow Jones index began 1973 at 1020 following a long rise. Then war broke out in the Middle East, oil prices quadrupled, Nixon resigned, and inflation hit 12.2% in the US. The Dow finished the year at 616. Over here, the FT100 Index touched 146 on January 6th 1975, and Burmah Oil went bust. The market then quickly rebounded and doubled in three months, while inflation touched 25% in 1975. It was a wild time and, understandably, some of our investment clients became very nervous, just as the banking clients had been. Once again, however, we performed well in the difficult conditions and held onto our clients, while our funds under management steadily grew.

We had a number of profitable and memorable clients on the banking side. I was introduced to Rupert Galliers

A Shaky Start and a Lot of Luck

Pratt, who had gained control of a pawn broking firm called Harvey and Thompson. Rupert came into the office and explained how pawnbrokers worked, and it struck me that as financial institutions go, it would be difficult to find anything safer. The average loan size was very small and secured against jewellery deposited with the lender, and usually the loan is repaid very quickly, typically within two to three months. Moreover, the rate of interest on an annualised basis was high, usually well in excess of 40%, and pawnbrokers don't need depositors. The only problem was that it was difficult to grow the business because people will normally borrow from conventional and cheaper sources of money, if at all possible. Harvey and Thompson had an established business; Rupert had a significant shareholding and it was also a quoted company. We bought a lot of shares which, in due course rose a great deal, responding to more effective management. Unfortunately, Rupert then diversified into consumer finance and other much riskier fields and the company soon got into trouble. By then, however, we were out. Eventually, Harvey Thompson was again spun out and sold for about £20 million.

Another client was Doxfords. This was a commodity broker with three partners: Michael Doxford, Nick Peto and Jake Morley. These were highly flamboyant characters who for a time made a great deal of money and they became useful clients. We had to be wary, nevertheless, because they did take substantial positions in various commodities. Nick Peto has written a book in which, among many amusing anecdotes, he gives an account of a pretty

Australian girl working for them as a secretary. Her first job in the mornings was to climb a ladder and mark up all the latest commodity prices on a large whiteboard. The three partners used to arrange their chairs near the bottom of the ladder and enjoyed looking up to see the view. In due course, Michael offered her a 10% salary increase on condition that she didn't wear any knickers. She would have had fun in the courts nowadays pursuing an anti-sexist case against her employers!

Dunbar may have had some colourful clients, but the lending policies of the bank were very strict, and we had the most excellent banking manager, Ted Coltman, who became a director in 1980. Ted came from Potters Bar, a suburb in north London which he was fond of describing as 'really delightful'. He was extremely careful with the bank's money, and it probably was as much due to his sound lending policies as to David's management of the creditors, that we managed to avoid the worst pitfalls of the 1970s. In 1980 the company was recapitalised and Dunbar went public; dealings in our shares commenced on the unlisted securities market. This followed a placing of 100,000 new £1 shares at £3 per share, and the distribution to existing shareholders of 200,000 bonus shares. We made £562,000 in the year to 31 December, beating our prospectus forecast, and an increase of 39% over the previous year. Dunbar was growing up!

In 1982 Dunbar obtained a full listing for its shares on the stock exchange, having made the transfer from the unlisted securities market and, in September, ten years after investing in Dunbar, we received an approach from

A Shaky Start and a Lot of Luck

Mark Weinberg, the founder of Hambro Life, who made an offer for Dunbar amounting to £10,000,000, which we accepted. It was quite an achievement that, in 10 years, we had increased profits from £75,000 to £802,000, with earnings per share up from 6p to 34.1p and assets up from 106p to 219p.

Mark had had to give up the Hambro name and was looking around for a new name which sounded respectable, and he also wanted a bank. We were just the right size and he knew David socially. It wasn't a great price, but it was always going to be a difficult business to grow and, considering all the risks we ran in the early seventies at the time of the fringe bank crisis, we thought it was worth accepting. Subsequently, Allied Dunbar has become a substantial business and the Dunbar name lives on.

The purchase and sale of Dunbar illustrates a rule that I have developed in my business career. When the shares in a company are falling heavily, it is worth having a close look. Mostly they are falling for good reasons and should be avoided but, occasionally, babies are being thrown out with the bathwater, and there is a good underlying business available very cheap. The old adage 'Buy things from frightened people and sell them to greedy ones,' always applies. At Dunbar, David and I paid too much for our shares; the board in 1973 were incredibly lucky to find two investors prepared to subscribe new capital at a full market price. They were certainly insufficiently frightened! Then, having built up a solid business over ten years, with a good profit record, we sold out too cheap. Those were two mistakes, but most of our rivals went bust, including some big banks. Mark was a shrewd purchaser; we should have sought a counter offer from a greedy one!

Contrary to public perception, banking is a highly risky business, which has again been borne out by the 2007/8 crash. The boards of Northern Rock and Halifax, Bank of Scotland (HBOS) for example, certainly neglected the first principles of sound banking and paid the price. It is also very hard to make money just from banking, without a fee-earning contribution. It was miraculous that Dunbar survived the fringe bank crisis, and we did a good job thereafter in building it up. Hambro Life bought it from us in very good shape.

However, throughout the 10 years I was working at Dunbar, a significant proportion of my time was also spent on a new company in which I had invested, Applied Computer Techniques, or ACT.

Chapter Eleven
ACT

During my years at Singer and Friedlander, a meeting took place which was to completely transform my business career for fifteen years. Singer and Friedlander had been approached by a young entrepreneur called Roger Foster who had set up a company, Applied Computer Techniques (ACT), which needed finance to expand. ACT, exactly as the name implied, ran computerised payrolls and ledgers for companies too small to afford their own computer. Singers weren't interested because the company was too small and risky, but I was intrigued by what they were doing, and impressed with Roger Foster. There were in fact three founders: Roger, the entrepreneur, was a qualified accountant working for GKN, Philip Smith, was the software architect, and Michael Nightingale, who also worked for GKN. Michael's family were in textiles and were the original backers. ACT's offices were directly across the road from Singer and Friedlander in the Hagley Road. I liked the idea of investing in computer-related businesses, and relished the opportunity of becoming more closely involved with the companies in which I invested. Up to now, these had all been established firms with a stock exchange listing, and I felt that an early stage, hands-on involvement, would be more fulfilling, albeit nerve-racking and risky.

ACT had developed their own computer software packages which, in the 1960s, was a new concept. These packages enabled any number of client companies to run payrolls, sales ledger, and other basic business applications on common standardised software. Nowadays, thousands of companies offer software packages but in the 1960s it was a novelty. The company could not afford its own computer, and they therefore leased time on an ICT mainframe computer at English Sewing Cotton in Manchester. Data collected from clients, mainly in the Midlands, had to be punched onto paper tape during the day, and then driven up to Manchester every evening to be processed overnight. This was the only time ACT could use a mainframe computer at a cost-effective rate. Costs were kept down by using a multi-company run, which reduced set up time per client dramatically; as with printing, the actual running time for each client company was short. It was the setting up of the program that took the time. ACT's unique ability to set up several companies on one program enabled them to offer competitive prices. A breakthrough opportunity arose for the young company when they attracted interest from two large companies in the Midlands, SC Larkins, the general wholesaler, and Edgar Vaughan, a distribution company, both of whom wanted to install a computerised sales and invoicing system. However, this required ACT to virtually double in size and, to service the new customer base effectively, they needed to lease their own computer. It was for this that the company needed an outside investor. By the end of 1967, before I made my investment, ACT had acquired 80 clients paying over £1,000 a month and after two years of losses, the company had just become profitable.

I felt it was a good bet. I commissioned an accountants'

report, and retained the services of the aforementioned Theo Christophers of the Birmingham law firm, Ryland Martineau. Against the advice of my peers at Singers, I then bought 25% of ACT for an investment of £12,500. This was the beginnings of a partnership with Roger Foster which lasted over 25 years and was the most important business decision of my life. Soon the company was to require further finance. There were two problems, first the large sums required to purchase capital equipment to develop and enhance the packages, and secondly the fact that the company, in selling its packages, incurred sizeable upfront selling and marketing costs, which were only recovered gradually by the monthly receipts from the clients. Before long, I was putting in further cash and signing bank guarantees, although at this stage I did not demand any further equity. The company was by now trading profitably, but Roger's ambitions were also growing and we were continually short of cash. Before long we were attracting the attention of other companies in the computer industry, notably Kode International, who expressed interest in making an offer for us. Roger wrote a letter to Mike Stoddart at the time…

> 'The steadying influence and advice of Lindsay Bury has been of growing value over the past 18 months. In addition Lindsay has provided further finance when required without any revamping of the share capital. In all fairness however he cannot be expected to continue to support ACT alone in the future while other non-executive shareholders contribute nothing; it is

the realisation of these facts that makes me on balance favourably disposed towards an outright sale.'

Kode then made an offer for £360,000, worth millions today, with £135,000 in cash and the remainder in Kode shares. There was no industrial logic in a sale to Kode, which manufactured computer peripherals and Roger and I much preferred to remain independent. He would never have been happy working for somebody else and I wanted to make a big profit, which Kode were not offering. We therefore decided to reject. It was a difficult decision that brought about the resignation of Philip Smith from the company. However, when in 1995 a book about ACT was written, Kode was still a public company capitalised in the region of £7,500,000 as against ACT's £200,000,000. It proved to be a good decision.

Following the rejection of the Kode offer, ACT began making steady profits and we expanded, setting up offices in Bristol. Two further offers were received for the company, but the prices were not tempting and, in any case, we didn't want to sell. In the year to March 1975, pre-tax profits were £90,000, compared with £62,000 the previous year and turnover, represented in the most part by monthly payments from customers using the bureau services, was £870,000 up from £640,000. A dividend of £4 a share was paid (this sounds hefty but there were only about 1,150 shares in issue), the company was already beginning to prepare for life as a public company and, for the first time, I issued a chairman's statement with our annual figures. The economic background in the country could hardly be less helpful, with the fringe bank crisis and the stock market crash still fresh in investor's minds throughout the seventies, and inflation reaching 25%. Nonetheless, in 1976 ACT's profits rose to £113,000 on turnover up to £1,079,490.

Further initiatives within the company took place, the most important being the establishment of ACT Financial Systems. This involved the installation on customers' premises of minicomputers, with a range of mainly financial applications, written by us. A feasibility study was carried out to decide on the customer's need for a computer, and the model best suited. The customer usually awarded the contract to source the hardware to ACT. Thus we supplied both the hardware, costing between £30,000 – £40,000, and the software, costing between £15,000 – £20,000. The hardware was bought by ACT from US manufacturers, mainly Digital Equipment Corporation, at a discount of 17½ to 20%. The most important application was an investment management package called Quasar, which was designed by ACT in collaboration with Dunbar, who became one of the earliest customers. Dunbar, where I was a director and in charge of the investment department, collaborated in writing the specification for the software, and a highly successful package resulted. We found that Quasar transformed Dunbar's business. ACT systems proved robust, flexible and cost-effective for the customers, and Quasar sold to many firms in the City, including Cazenove. ACT systems could expand rapidly because, unlike the bureau business, selling and installation costs were fully recovered up front from the sale, which benefited both profitability and cash flow. This became the highly profitable division which, in the latter part of ACT's existence in the eighties and nineties, was the mainstay of the whole business.

In 1978 preparations were in full swing to get a public listing. Pre-tax profits had risen in the year to March 1977 to £247,000 and, by December 1978, this figure had already been exceeded and the forecast for the full year to March 1979 was for profits of not less than £360,000. The principal shareholders in the group were myself with 27½%, Roger with 18.3%, and the other directors with a further 15%. The actual flotation of the company took place under rule 163/2 and was an enormous success; the placing price was 95p and the issue was handled by my old colleagues at Singer and Friedlander, with Timothy Harford at the helm. On the day of the placing, the shares rose to 150p by lunchtime, ending the day at 175-180p. Results for the year to March 1979 brought profits up by 51% to £372,000, comfortably above the £360,000 forecast in the flotation prospectus. I still remember waking up in the middle of the night after the first day of dealings, and calculating that my shareholding was worth over £600,000 and thinking that, for the first time in my life, I had made some real money. I could hardly believe it. The real excitement in ACT, however, was yet to come; by the summer of 1980 profits had risen to £720,000 and the greatest opportunity was just round the corner.

The next phase of the story begins in the autumn of 1978, when we were approached by an unusual entrepreneur, Julian Allason, with the suggestion that we might like to buy his company Petsoft Microcomputer Software. Allason was the son of an MP, and the brother of Rupert Allason, Conservative Member of Parliament for Torbay, with a sideline of writing spy thrillers under the name of Nigel West. Julian had for a long time been involved in marketing consumer electronics, and he went out to the USA to look at the Commodore PET (Personal Electronic Transactor), one of the first microcomputers to appear on world markets. Commodore had been set up by Jack Tramiel, a survivor of one of Hitler's concentration camps, but the designer who developed the PET was a man named Chuck Peddle.

Julian immediately realised the potential of the new microcomputers, and the PET in particular, but also appreciated they would be useless without application programs. He therefore built up a wide range of software, sourced from independent authors, with a library of nearly 250 programs, prominent among which were an accounts program selling at £12, Mathspack at £12, and Microchess at £14. Demand exploded, and the company enjoyed immediate strong sales growth with very healthy profit margins.

Julian and his wife, Jessica, were running the business from their home, a farmhouse in Yattendon in Berkshire, packaging up the tapes on their kitchen table. While costs were very low, they were unable to cope with the demands of very rapid growth and Julian decided he needed a partner. He kept hearing the name of ACT, which interested him, and he organised an introduction to me through Rupert Galliers Pratt, a friend, and also a Dunbar client.

ACT

I introduced him to Roger, and Roger tried to play chess against the PET program and was defeated. Various combinations and forms of collaboration were discussed until, following a visit down to Yattendon, it was agreed that ACT should acquire the business. We signed the deal on 1st January 1979, with a down payment of £40,000 and a royalty of 10% of net turnover in excess of £10,000 a month for 2 years. One of our directors, Peter Oldershaw, was seconded to Berkshire, where he lived in the Royal Oak pub for three months, while the sales operation was moved from Allason's kitchen to an adjacent barn. They had to send so many registered parcels that he was forced to tour other local village post offices each day, so that they could cope with the volume. After three months, everything was moved to ACT.

Meanwhile, Julian travelled regularly to California and got to know Bill Gates and the founders of Apple, Steve Jobs and Steve Wozniak, and it was from his contacts in California that ACT signed up the UK rights for Visicalc, the world's first micro spreadsheet, and generally extended his contacts in Silicon Valley. Petsoft was incredibly profitable but its future was limited; the PET's keyboard was primitive and cassettes, with all the winding and rewinding, would soon be made obsolete by the introduction of floppy disks.

Petsoft was a good investment by any standards, but its most important legacy was in leading ACT to the US and the legendary Chuck Peddle, who had developed the revolutionary PET computer. He had started in the electronics industry in the early 1970s and had worked for

Motorola, designing their leading edge 68000 processor. He disagreed with their pricing policy and left to join a virtually unknown company, MOS Technology, in Valley Forge, Pennsylvania. While at MOS and developing the 6502 chip, Peddle built into it many of the features that could be used in a personal computer. MOS, short of cash, were not interested in developing it and Peddle approached Jack Tramiel, boss of office furniture manufacturer, Commodore. Tramiel was skeptical, but suggested Peddle build a prototype to show at an office equipment exhibition. The computer was called PET, Personal Electronic Transactor; it used Microsoft Basic language and integral screen, cassette and a calculator type keyboard. Peddle had discussed the PET with his friend, Bill Gates, who had recently formed a company called Microsoft. After unsuccessful approaches to Apple and Tandy, Peddle continued his discussions with Tramiel at Commodore, finally concluding a deal that resulted in the development of the highly successful Commodore PET, which rapidly became a market leader. However, he was a restless man and he really wanted to develop a second-generation machine, which Commodore was unwilling to finance, and so he moved on, followed in true American style, by a flurry of writs from Tramiel.

Meanwhile, Julian Allason had got to know Peddle and introduced him to Roger Foster. ACT in the UK had already become the most successful vendor of software for the Commodore PET. Peddle was therefore keen on the 'limeys', as he called us, and found ACT a 'switched on group of guys'. Allason got his permission to show us Peddle's new

ACT

machine, shortly to be called Sirius. A demo took place to Foster and the ACT management team.

We were very excited and immediately saw the possibilities. The Sirius was genuinely revolutionary: not only was it 16 bit as opposed to 8 bit and consequently much faster than anything on the market but with high resolution graphics and inbuilt discs and considerable memory capacity, it was probably two years ahead of the competition. In Roger Foster's view, it is only every few years that a truly stunning product appears on the market. Sirius was one, the Apple II was another, and the DEC VAX was yet another. Roger flew to California to see Chuck and look at the prototypes being developed, over a drink in Norm's Bar in Scotts Valley, and we requested exclusive distribution rights in the UK for ACT. Peddle was interested, but wanted a guarantee that we would take 2,500 computers in the first year. ACT was now a public company; nevertheless, a commitment to 2,500 of an unproven machine retailing at £2,395 was a major step. It was one of those moments when taking a calculated risk could bring a huge leap forward for the company. Roger dispatched his senior management team to see if they shared his excitement, which they did, and the commitment was made.

The Sirius was then launched at the Dorchester in London, in the autumn of 1981, under the slogan 'Seeing is believing' and. within a few months, over 700 dealers placed orders (with a minimum of three machines and payment up front), and were clamouring for supplies. The launch was followed by a highly successful television

A Shaky Start and a Lot of Luck

advertising campaign, the first ACT had ever undertaken. Microcomputer Printout magazine reviewed the Sirius comprehensively, and pointed out that Sirius was not a copy or an upgrade of the PET. For one thing, it was based on a completely different microprocessor, the Intel 8088, and it also had a different approach to memory, with 128 bytes of RAM as standard, and two built-in floppy disk drives with 1.2 million bytes of online storage. Furthermore, the screen display achieved a new standard, with the capability of 132 characters across the screen, sufficient for a complete set of budgets. Finally, Peddle and his team had addressed seriously the ergonomics of the Sirius, an area often treated casually by other computer designers, notably IBM! The monitor could be rotated through an angle of 42° and tilted up to 11°, and the screen was fitted with an antiglare optical filter to ease eyestrain. The keyboard was freestanding, connected to the computer box by a coiled lead and with long travel keys; even the screen brightness and contrast could be controlled from the keyboard. It was a phenomenal product.

The success of Sirius was so great that it immediately dwarfed everything else in the company. We established a network of over 200 main dealers and were selling thousands of machines, to everyone's relief; it had, after all, been bought off the drawing board. It proved to be totally reliable, and also attracted a wealth of software development. Indeed, we quickly registered over 250 third-party software products; interest from software authors and systems houses had been intense. The basic commercial software, financial modelling, Visicalc,

ACT

Micromodeller and WordStar, had all been released to dealers. We had no competitor in Britain and, indeed, US sales of Sirius lagged far behind the UK. ACT decided to launch a rights issue in June 1982, to assist further growth. We had by then achieved a fourfold increase in sales and profits since we went public in 1979.

In May 1982, James Capel, a major London stockbroker, produced a comprehensive 33-page survey on the company concluding...

> *'ACT is a fundamentally attractive stock with strong management, a healthy balance sheet and a good performance record; recent moves will turn the group into a highly integrated small business systems supplier with around two thirds sales exposure to the very high growth microcomputer sector. Profits are expected to increase dramatically in 1982/3 due to the new Sirius 1 microcomputer which is achieving better-than-expected results. At the current price of 190p we do not think that the serious prospects have yet been fully discounted in the share price. We continue to recommend this stock.'*

By mid-1982, the market was aware that ACT's profits from the Sirius would outstrip anything seen earlier. The historic price earnings ratio for the stock was a Japanese-style 52.7, with a gross yield of 0.4%; clearly not a share for widows and orphans. (This did not stop me recommending them to everyone! A close friend, Virginia Storey, was able to buy a beautiful oil painting of one of her ancestors, from the profits on her ACT stock)

A Shaky Start and a Lot of Luck

Competition was clearly going to be ferocious in such a high-growth market. The IBM Micro had launched in the US but it had less memory, lower capacity disk drives, and less powerful graphics. It was also a bulky unattractive box and overpriced; if it sold in the UK at the same price as in the US, it would be £3,000 against £2,395 for the Sirius. ACT had managed to get the three essentials for explosive growth: a breakthrough product, a sensational price, and brilliant marketing.

In the month of December 1982, ACT sold 1,000 Sirius machines and Chuck Peddle flew in from California saying, 'I promised these guys a no-expense-spared party once they hit the thousand a month mark. I figured we would be partying in the spring but our friends evidently fancied a pre-Christmas celebration.'

Chuck Peddle was a highly charismatic and entertaining character, and a genius at computer design. However, his management style was, to put it mildly, eccentric. He was the sole boss of Sirius, with no proper senior management. He had no conception of delegation, and didn't believe in sleep. When he came over to the UK, which was often, he would head for the Playboy Club with a large roll of £50 notes and, when he wasn't gambling, he was taking telephone calls from his management team in California between 2 and 3am at the tables. I remember vividly a meeting in the offices of the lawyers Clifford Chance in the City. We were discussing an important deal recasting the relationship between Sirius and ACT; it was a big meeting with about fifteen people in the room. Chuck had brought over from California an attractive girl who had been a dancer, but was described by Chuck as his lawyer. She didn't make any contribution to the discussion, but he stood behind her chair throughout the meeting massaging her neck. There were a large number of people around the table, including the then senior partner of Clifford Chance. The lawyers droned on interminably, and both Chuck and his nubile young lawyer were showing signs of impatience. I remember him calling the senior partner 'an asshole', which took this very senior lawyer aback somewhat. Before long, leaving one of his minions to tie up the loose ends, Chuck and his lady lawyer headed off to the Playboy Club. Clubbing and jogging were his main enthusiasms which, allied to being a genius at computer design, made for an unusual skill set!

Increasingly, however, we were becoming uneasy about ACT's huge reliance upon Sirius, whose day-to-day management was not good, and decision-making increasingly erratic. To illustrate Chuck's unusual management style, we heard that after he was sacked from Victor, Sirius's parent company, people to whom he had offered jobs kept arriving at the company for months after he left. He had no HR department and had failed to tell anyone, or to keep a record of the fact that he had offered them jobs. Roger believed that it was only a matter of time before something went seriously wrong and we had an interruption in supplies. We just couldn't afford to risk this and so in the autumn of 1982, the ACT board came to a momentous decision. We decided to manufacture our own computer.

Chapter Twelve
Apricot

The decision to make our own computer was a daring and risky step and, years later with the benefit of hindsight, we were told by some that we should never have gone into manufacturing. We were betting the company on it. But it could also be argued that to do nothing was also betting the company. Sirius was now the core of ACT's profits, and the company needed certainty of supply and a strong pipeline of attractive future products. Sirius was a world-beating product and we had a highly attractive distribution agreement. Nothing comparable would be available from any other manufacturer, even if they had equivalent products, which they did not. There was also a strong likelihood that Sirius would be taken over, which would almost certainly jeopardise our distribution agreement. To make our own machine seemed much the best option.

Cautiously, over a period of months, we recruited a design team and put together a specification, which incorporated many of the best features of the Sirius and was, of course, entirely software compatible with it, but which also incorporated several advances in technology, enabling a better display, a smaller case with 3.5 inch discs, using tried and tested components with a single board design. It was also built to sell at a significantly lower price. The current retail price of a 16-bit PC was then around £2,400 which, with software, would cost in the region of £3,500. The equivalent configuration with our product was budgeted to retail from £1,495. We would

Apricot

standardise on the MS-DOS operating system from Microsoft. We already had 300 Sirius dealers and were expecting the number to increase to 500 by the middle of 1983. We could make a profit just by satisfying the home demand, ignoring exports, which, as a manufacturer, we were now free to develop.

We recruited a top computer designer, Peter Horne, from Philips. Peter would work with the software supplier, Microsoft, to make sure that the new computer, codenamed Apricot, was compatible with the Sirius. With an installed base of over 20,000 Sirius PCs already sold in the UK and a large library of software, this seemed more essential than compatibility with IBM at the time. We had to be compatible with Sirius; whether we would have simultaneously been able to also achieve compatibility with IBM is doubtful. The name Apricot was a loose acronym of Applied Computer Techniques and, of course, it was a bit of a play on the competitor, Apple. Fruity computers seemed to be in fashion.

As the project moved along, a development committee met every Friday, chaired by Roger Foster with Peter Horne, and a number of other key executives. It was a race against time; we had to be on the market in the autumn, a mere nine months after pressing the button to go ahead.

The next question was: where should we build the computer. The UK was the obvious place, and we started to look around urgently for a factory. After extensive investigation, we settled on a site in Glenrothes in Fifeshire, Scotland, an old coal mining area across the Firth of Forth, north east of Edinburgh. We received a great deal of help from the Glenrothes Development Corporation (GDC), and there was a pool of skilled electronics labour in this area, following the closure of a Burroughs factory, a large American computer company. The GDC were model partners and they were aware of our deadlines and bent over backwards to help. Martin Cracknell, the CEO wrote:

> *'It was a most exhilarating experience for all of us to meet you and your team last week. I wish that every potential client company was as dynamic, open, professional and friendly as yours. It is too much to hope that they would have a project half as exciting. You certainly turned us all on!'*

This was in March and, by 31 August, the 20,000 ft² extension and all external work were completed, and the factory was ready.

By the beginning of March, ACT were able to announce they were going to manufacture their own computer. The *Financial Times* commented:

> *'The highflying British computer group Applied Computer Techniques again demonstrated its ability to stand out from the crowd with a £6 million rights issue to fund a new microcomputer. ACT has been storming the UK market for personal computers with a powerful 16 bit Sirius machine which has had a dramatic effect on ACT's growth.'*

It was only eight months since the company had last asked its shareholders for extra funds, but the intervening period had seen the most rapid growth in the company's history and, clearly, entering into manufacturing was going to require further money. 2,246,062 new shares were issued on a 1 for 5 basis at 280p a share, raising £6.05 million. The issue was underwritten by Singer and Friedlander. We were already beginning to get mutterings from the City that we were issuing too many shares. However, it is as well that we did, because it was due to our conservative funding policy that the company was able to survive the storms that lay ahead. Meanwhile, the market seemed quite happy as the shares rose up 40p to 400p which was 44 times the fully taxed prospective earnings of 83p, offering a prospective yield of 0.5%. The market were not the only people to be happy. When we achieved full production, we created 400 jobs in our Scottish factory. George Younger, the Secretary of State for Scotland, announced: 'It is yet another first for Scotland. This decision confirms that Scotland has the right infrastructure and workforce to attract this type of project.'

ACT was the sort of company that in the midst of the economic gloom, displayed a can-do approach, which was uplifting to all who became involved. In March 1983 we released our results showing profits more than doubled at £2,168,000, and more than forecast at the time of the rights issue back in March. The City reacted well and the shares jumped a further 22p to 497p. Above all, our new machine was a fantastic product.

This was the view of no less a man than Bill Gates, head of Microsoft and now one of the richest men in the world. He attended a meeting we set up in London and was genuinely impressed; this was a state-of-the-art machine, with all the latest software and features of the Apple Lisa, selling at a fraction of the price, and he particularly liked the fact that it ran MS-DOS and was thus firmly in the Microsoft camp. It had twin 3.5 inch discs and really looked elegant and stylish; a complete contrast to the IBM PC, which looked boring and was overpriced.

What was the attitude of Sirius to the launch of Apricot? Chuck Peddle at first expressed guarded approval of ACT's launch of its own microcomputer, but the reality was that it was going to be competitive as well as complementary. The Sirius, with its larger storage through the Winchester disk options, and larger screen and keyboard, should in theory not be affected by the lower-priced portable Apricots. In fact, if Apricots were to be as successful as the City hoped, it would almost certainly have a detrimental effect on sales of Sirius through ACT and, before long, Apricot would move upmarket and the two companies would be competing head to head. For ACT, it was vital to do a deal with Peddle: until the sales of Apricot built up, the last thing we wanted was for Peddle to switch supplies of the Sirius direct to the dealers, thereby cutting out ACT. Negotiations ran on right up to the launch of Apricot and, as so often in deals with American companies, became bogged down between the lawyers.

Finally, on the very eve of the launch, Chuck and Roger decided they should sort things out over dinner. At midnight they left the lawyers' offices and went to Langan's Brasserie in Mayfair, at that time highly fashionable. Between midnight and 2am, they thrashed out an agreement, including the different positioning of the Sirius

Apricot

and the new Apricot in the marketplace. The Sirius was to be the desktop computer while the Apricot was to be the portable. This agreement was of critical importance to ACT, as it enabled the company to continue selling Sirius whilst it built up deliveries of Apricots.

In Scotland, ACT in fact carried out only a limited amount of real manufacturing. We were primarily an assembly plant, bringing in 140 different components sourced from all over the world. The keyboard, for example, came from KeyTronics in the USA, the disk drives from Sony, the Winchester disc drives from Rodime in Glenrothes, and the main processor board, although designed by ACT, was manufactured in the Far East. All were subjected to quality control batch testing, before being accepted into stock. ACT released its interim figures to September 1983 and, as had been anticipated, turnover and profits more than doubled; in my chairman's statement, I was highly optimistic about the future. Noting that 1,000 Apricots had been delivered in the first month of production and the order book exceeded 10,000, I said that there was every sign that the Apricots would establish a significant presence in world markets.

Sales of Apricots continued to climb throughout 1983 and, in the year to March 1984, turnover raced ahead to £50 million and profits to £4.64 million. In June 1984 ACT had a tremendous promotion at the Albert Hall; 2,500 dealers and distributors from all over the world were invited, as well as dancing girls and entertainers, Ronnie Corbett and Ned Sherrin. They introduced some light relief to the deadly serious business of introducing ACT's latest additions to the Apricot range, the F1 and the portable. Once again our products were well received and analysts were expecting ACT to double sales in 1984 to beyond £100 million, and treble profits to around £14 million. At that time, following our trading success and the two rights issues, we had £20 million in cash in the bank. Even the *Wall Street Journal* were impressed and reckoned that the prediction of Apple's Steve Jobs, that ACT and other small Apple competitors would get wiped out this year, was unlikely to be fulfilled. In September, it was announced that Barson Computers Pty, ACT's Australian distributor, had won a major contract to supply the agricultural department of the New South Wales government with 3,000 Apricots. This deal, plus others overseas, led ACT to believe that the decision to invest in manufacturing, in order to overcome the restriction to the UK market that the Sirius agreement had imposed, had been totally correct. I gave an interview to *Computer News*, exalting our new ability to export.

> *'As distributors we were faced with two probable fates; if we did well we would be taken over and if we did badly we would be fired.'*

Now, those things didn't have to happen.

Chapter Thirteen
Disaster

One of the major decisions facing any fast-growing British company is what to do about the US market. Clearly, we were now in a position where we could export, since we manufactured our own product and we were already achieving success in other export markets. However, an additional opportunity suddenly presented itself. Apple in the US had acquired a new chief executive, John Sculley from Pepsi-Cola. According to his autobiography, Jobs managed to lure him from Pepsi with the line, 'Do you want to go on flogging sugared water for the rest of your life or do you want to change the world?'

It proved a seductive pitch, and Sculley joined Apple – only to sack Jobs a few years later. Before then, however, he decided that Apple's route to market in the USA should be changed, and notice was served on fifteen major distributors in the United States, terminating their contracts. This would leave a substantial hole in the sales of all these companies, and they badly needed a replacement product.

They formed themselves into what they called a National Sales Organisation and came over to see us in Birmingham, where they spent nearly a week looking at our products. I vividly remember learning about the size and potential of the US market from these characters, who came from New York, Chicago, Atlanta, Denver, and most of the other main centres in the US. They appeared to like the Apricot very much, and an agreement was reached whereby ACT would have access to 250 dealers across the US by January

Disaster

1985. No binding contracts were signed, but we were sufficiently encouraged by this and other market indicators to decide to set up a separate company, Apricot Inc, to exploit this opportunity in the USA. We did not, however, wish to expose our UK shareholders to the full risk of our entry into the US, and we looked around for a sound and conservative method of financing for the new company. Once again, the admirable Tim Harford from Singer and Friedlander came up with a solution. An issue was made of $20,000,000 of stock, of which 30 % was placed with financial institutions, 51% offered for subscription with preference given to existing ACT shareholders, and ACT itself subscribed for the remainder. When the new company reached a sufficient level of profitability, it was to be floated as a separate entity and, in the meantime, Singer and Friedlander would make a market in the shares. ACT had an option to buy back 40% of the shares it did not own, which would give control. On the other hand, crucially, if the venture failed the dilution of ACT's own equity would be restricted to 9.2%. It was an adroit response to an extraordinary opportunity presented by the deal with the Apple distribution chain and other overseas opportunities.

If 1984 was ACT's year of triumph, 1985 proved to be to be one of trial. In our results to 31 March 1985, we had demonstrated the growth which we had led our supporters to expect, with turnover up by 82% to £92.4 million, and profits by 130% to £10.65 million. Our margins had also increased from 9.1% to 11.5%. Nevertheless, the stock market was worried and our shares fell from a rights-

A Shaky Start and a Lot of Luck

adjusted 280p at the beginning of the year to 160p by the time the year's results were released in the middle of June. In the US, Apricot got off to a very slow start. The magazine *Creative Computing* gave our product a good review. Unfortunately, enquiries could not be followed up with immediate deliveries as we did not receive the two necessary electrical product approvals and, by the time these were forthcoming, competitive machines had appeared and interest had cooled. We also had some upsets in the US management, with a number of senior people leaving. Sales never achieved critical mass and after 14 months of operation Apricot Inc had made sales of just $4 million, a long way short of the $1 million a month level, forecast by John Leftwich, our marketing director. Before long it became clear that it would require too much money to build up Apricot to a viable level, and the company was sold off to two Apricot employees. It was an abject failure, reflecting gross under-preparation for the huge task of getting established in the US market.

Before long we began to attract the attention of the press, only this time their interest was less flattering. On 13 October 1985 *The Sunday Times* computer specialist, Jane Bird wrote an article that caused us a lot of problems, quoting some very inaccurate market share figures. *The Observer* also wrote an article two weeks later:

> 'The real concern for most computer buyers must be Apricot's lack of true IBM compatibility. Apricot is faced with a dilemma; it can make its machines IBM-compatible and thus become yet another manufacturer of IBM PC clones or it can

Disaster

stick to its (some say, superior) architecture and go it alone which is risky and may mean contraction.'

This article had, indeed, identified the heart of our problem. IBM had launched its own personal computer, which was generally regarded as a boring, overpriced machine with limited functionality, but it had the magic letters IBM on the box. Back in the mid eighties, 90% of businesses, particularly in the US, wanted an IBM or IBM-compatible machine. We were a victim of our early success. We had established market leadership in the UK and had achieved extraordinary success but in 1985, after several months of disappointing sales, both in the UK and elsewhere, we became convinced that ACT had to become IBM-compatible. The trouble was, first, this had to be done in secrecy in order not to affect the existing sales of our current product range. Secondly, we were going to have to make a huge provision against stocks of computers and components made obsolete by the decision to go IBM-compatible. In June 1986, I had to announce a loss of £15.4 million, nearly all of which was due to stock write-offs, although our operating profits had also fallen to £4.2 million from £10.6 million the previous year. The share price fell to 54p before recovering a little to 69p, and it was back to where it had been at the beginning of 1982 before the Sirius/Apricot excitement started. We had to announce redundancies in the company and the resignation of several directors. The sole redeeming feature was that we did not go bust. We had always financed the company highly conservatively, most notably with the way we put Apricot Inc together, and this long-standing caution undoubtedly saved us. The directors of ACT, principally Roger and myself, did do a placing of a portion of our own shares at 230p; so we did sell out part of our holdings near the top.

Looking back, with the benefit of hindsight, I don't think we should have done anything differently. Chuck Peddle and Sirius took us into the big time and we became a major British computer company, the first to go public since ICL. We established Sirius and later Apricot as the bestselling small business computers in the UK, and increasingly were achieving success in overseas markets. With this large customer base wedded to our architecture, it was not possible to be an IBM-compatible vendor as well as supporting our Sirius/Apricot architecture. We had to choose and, of course, we were committed to our existing customers. At the same time, few managements would have walked away from the opportunity presented by the Apple dealers to enter the US market, particularly as we had found such a neat way of financing it. Our fault lay in grossly underestimating the task of getting established in the US, to which we did not even begin to devote enough resource. I do not think we could or should have ducked the opportunity; we were defeated by the emergence of the IBM software standard, and the arrival of a tidal wave of new competitors from the US and the Far East, making IBM clones. With the exception of IBM and Apple, most of these went bust or were taken over. Wang, Data General and Compaq went bust and even DEC, one of the most valuable companies in the world, sold out a year or two later for a song.

It is astonishing how ruthless competition in the

Disaster

computer industry has devoured so many companies. Literally over a twelve-month period hardware became a commodity. Somehow we survived this hurricane blowing through our industry. We did this by going back to our roots as a software company.

Chapter Fourteen
Life at Millichope – Filling up the House

At the time all these excitements were going on in Birmingham, Sarah and I were living in Millichope and bringing up our young family, which consisted of Frank, born in 1970, and Harriet in 1972. We were also very busy at home during this time. The garden we had inherited was enormous, comprising about 11 acres in total. When we moved in, we decided to fell about sixty nondescript spruce planted by the school, and began the process of making a new garden, building on the wonderful framework of large and majestic trees, the lake, and the temple that we'd inherited from previous generations. Sarah designed a new formal garden, built on the terrace to the south west of the house. This was on a small intimate scale, comprising three garden rooms enclosed by yew hedges. Lily ponds and in due course a swimming pool were integrated into this garden, together with a beautiful garden gate made in Dumfriesshire, which was a copy of a gate commissioned by Micky Ingall at Corsock. It was a delight to relax there on a summer evening after my long flog back from Birmingham. She also made a water garden which, though rewarding, was incredibly hard work; she was often to be seen waist-deep in the lake, removing aquatic weeds and other unwelcome residents.

Frank and Harriet in due course started school at the Munslow village school, a mile up the road, where they received a very good education and made friends with the children from up and down the valley.

Life at Millichope – Filling up the House

Inside the house we rattled around a bit at first because we had no furniture. My grandfather, after the war, had taken the view that no one ever again would be able to afford to live in stately homes so most of the furniture was sold although, happily, some of the better pictures, lent to the Shropshire County Council, we managed to recover. My sister Sara was entitled by inheritance to half the chattels, further reducing what was available for Millichope. Of the five main reception rooms, the music room and the drawing room had no furniture at all and the hall was empty, leaving the library, which mercifully still had the family books, although these were in poor condition. It also had mahogany pelmets beneath which we had draped some vast, expensive velour curtains. There we would watch television until it was time for the climb up to our bedroom on the first floor. We got used to these slightly spartan surroundings and the children and our friends and weekend guests, if they noticed at all, accepted that the house was somewhat under-furnished. We wanted to clutter the house up a bit but to have the time, the knowledge and energy to acquire very large objects suitable for the house was a daunting task.

It was in the mid 1970s that I sought the help of a friend and neighbour, Hew Kennedy from Acton Round. Hew is the eldest son of a remarkable woman, Bobbin Kennedy who, before the war, had been a girlfriend of my father's. From her, Hew inherited a taste for adventure and love of dangerous practical jokes, of which I was a victim on more than one occasion. He also inherited a farm which took up part of his time, but his main passion is fine art, including pictures and furniture, in which he dealt extensively, as

A Shaky Start and a Lot of Luck

well as armour, which he excelled in repairing and renovating. He now has also made a speciality in designing and making chandeliers.

I had a big problem with a large and empty house and no time to go to dealers and auction rooms, let alone develop the taste and eye required to build a collection. Hew began to make some suggestions. The first was a magnificent Coade stone lion weighing about a ton and standing on its plinth, about 5 feet high. This came up for sale at Sothebys, and I remember we paid £250 for it, plus a further £275 to the haulier to get it back to Shropshire. This was duly installed in the hall where it fitted magnificently; my collecting days had begun. A year or two later, Hew said there was a large country house sale taking place by order of the Morrison family, at Fonthill in Wiltshire. He particularly wanted me to buy a very large, Spanish parcel gilt chest, made by a metallurgist in the Basque Country in Spain, in the late-19th century, called Placido Zuloaga. Even from the catalogue, I could see that it was a magnificent object but I didn't have the time to go and inspect it. Hew, however, set off to Wiltshire and we agreed that we would bid up to £3,000. On the day of the sale I took a telephone call from him, which turned out to be one of the more important ones of my life. He said that Christopher Gibbs, the well-known London dealer, had bought it for a fraction over £3,000, and he recommended that we should give him an immediate profit by offering £4,000. Hew said that if Gibbs didn't have to move it back to London and could pocket an immediate profit of £1,000, a one-third profit on his outlay, it would be a good day's

Life at Millichope – Filling up the House

work. I agreed; our offer was accepted and the chest came back to Millichope.

Once there, it looked magnificent against the wall of the entrance hall, just by the front door. Already at Fonthill it had been very dirty (Peter Morrison subsequently told me that the family used to stack fishing rods on top of it) but Shropshire is an even damper county than Wiltshire, and the chest came from a much drier part of the world in northern Spain. Rust was the problem for the iron parts, which we tried to oil, and we used Duraglit to clean the silver parts and ammonia for the gold. However, most of our efforts were in vain, because visitors arriving through the front door would chuck their wet raincoats on it. It was a job to keep the rust off and this proved to be a continuing problem.

Then fifteen years later Hew rang to say that someone wanted to buy the chest. I wasn't keen to sell, because it looked splendid against the wall by the front door in the spot which we had found for it. Unusually, at that time I didn't need the money and it would leave a big gap on an important wall so I said, 'No'. Hew then became more specific; the mystery buyer was prepared to pay £250,000 for it. Although this was a fantastic profit, it came at a time when we had just floated ACT and I was feeling quite rich. I didn't need to sell furniture; indeed, I was much more interested in buying it. So I refused.

After another four years, Hew returned to the subject. He had a different message to convey: 'Was there any price at which Mr Bury would be prepared to sell his chest?'

Now this was more interesting; everything has a value

and I remember consulting Leon Brittan, by then a cabinet minister in Mrs Thatcher's government, who was staying for the weekend. I thought a touch of Jewish acumen wouldn't come amiss, and we all had a debate about how much I should ask. A figure of £400,000 was agreed, exactly one hundred times my purchase cost. Adopting the supermarketeer's coyness about round figures, I asked for £395,000. The offer was immediately accepted and the money was in my account at the end of the week. I was amazed; no attempt at a haggle and immediate payment! I wasn't used to this at all.

I subsequently discovered that the purchaser was an Iraqi called Dr Khalili. He had spent many years collecting items by Zuloaga, the world's foremost exponent of damascening precious metals on iron. An exhibition was about to take place at the Victoria and Albert Museum called, *'The Art and Tradition of the Zuloagas, featuring Spanish Damascene from the Khalili collection'.* My chest was to form the heart of his collection. He had over the years, bought about a hundred items by Zuloaga and he really had to have this chest, which was by far the largest and most important item, other than those in the possession of the Spanish Royal Family. I still possess the catalogue of the V&A exhibition and the chest takes up eight pages! Of course, I'd known nothing of all this and, indeed, was shamefully ignorant about the unique object that I had bought. I later became aware that Khalili in fact paid a great deal more than the sum paid to me, and Hew and the agent acting for him, received the difference as commission. I didn't begrudge them a penny, being very satisfied with

Life at Millichope – Filling up the House

the very large amount of money that I had received.

This coup now formed a war chest for purchases for the house, and I mentally allocated all proceeds to the task of furnishing Millichope. We had already made a start with an immense chandelier for the hall. The hall was very dark and poorly lit, and I had asked Hew for some time to look around for a really large chandelier. After a while he came back saying that he had been unable to find anything but that if I wasn't in a hurry he would make me one. I had learned to trust Hew and I asked him to sketch out roughly what he had in mind, which he did on the back of an envelope. It was a large elaborate affair with two big circular metal brackets connected by streamers and a great many bowls containing the lighting bulbs. It was a risky commission, but I had a hunch that Hew would come up with the goods. About six months later, he rang up saying that his stables were full of glass and would I like to come and look. There was, indeed, an astonishing amount of Indian glass, covering a large area of floor in his barn, which Hew disdainfully described as being of very bad quality. He then set about getting the metal brackets made, the lower of which weighed about three hundredweight, and then he found the streamer glass from Germany. Finally, it was assembled over a period of a month, with the aid of extensive scaffolding and the local electrician, Michael Lawrence, who wired the whole thing up for £500. It has one hundred and forty bowls containing the bulbs, and I know of no larger chandelier in a private house in Britain. It has been a remarkable success and lights the whole space brilliantly, looking particularly good from the hall below. From the gallery, a purist might be disappointed that the globes are not entirely even, but for the £15,000 Hew charged me, I was well satisfied.

Now, with the aid of Dr Khalili's largesse, other objects followed. Six very large Dutch paintings by Anthony and Jurriaan Andriessen had come on offer from the Getty Museum, who decided they needed the space for more valuable items. Hew bought them in rolls. I acquired four, which we deployed in the drawing room, and then I managed to find the missing two. One problem was that they were too large even for our drawing room. Hew's solution was simply to chop the tops off with the result that the trees disappear into the frame at the top of each picture. I still retain the tops and it doesn't seem to have made much, if any, difference to the value of the pictures and most people don't notice. This enabled us finally to decorate and furnish the drawing room - ten years after we had moved into the house. We acquired some pictures for the hall; a very large d'Hondecoeter hung over the lion, featuring 'a peacock, peahen, magpie, spaniel, cockerel and chickens by a ruined pedestal'. On either side appeared two classical landscapes by Orizzonte, whose real name was Jan Frans van Bloemen, featuring scenes from classical antiquity, beneath which stand a pair of late 17th century thrones in the style of Brustellon. These came from a set of twelve from Mentmore, originally from the Doges Palace in Venice, and were bought for me by Humphry Wakefield, a close friend from Cambridge.

The music room, which had been decorated by David Mlinaric in lilac and violet colours, had also been empty for ten years. For this room Hew found some 18th century Chinese hand-painted wallpapers from the Governor's house in Williamsburg, Virginia. The Americans had decided apparently that it was no longer appropriate for the Governor's house to be furnished in the European style, and they wanted to replace this look with authentically American items. Thus, the wallpapers were detached from the walls in sheets. Hew bought them and he and his family cut them up into panels. The overall effect is astonishingly good, combining wonderfully with the Mlinaric colour scheme in that room.

All this had been paid for from the proceeds of the Zuloaga chest, and since then further important items have appeared, made by the younger generation of the Kennedy family. A pair of gilt tables with scagliola tops, made by Tom Kennedy, Hew and Sue's eldest son, beneath which feature wooden gilded mermaids with long tails, hand mirrors and an assortment of lobsters and seaweed and other marine accessories. Tom's tops were inlaid in scagliola onto two slabs of granite; they depict numerous highly coloured fish swimming on top of the back granite, which gives the feel of very deep water. These tables stand on either side of the main staircase. Tom has since become the UK number-one craftsman in scagliola, and has made a huge panel of a rainforest for Sarah and me at our house in the village of Tugford, where we now live. The tables were entirely made by craftsmen in Shropshire, and this achievement was immortalised by a classics master in Shrewsbury school who composed a Latin commemoration of the tables' commissioning and construction; this appears

A Shaky Start and a Lot of Luck

in a frieze round the tops:

Has mensas ab Hugo Kennedy conceptas
A Calino Hawkins delineatas
A Ronaldo Hestair caelatas
A Carolo Manners auratas
A Thoma Kennedy in superficie marmoratas
Toto opera suis pecunis effecto
Ornamentum aedibus suis Millichope Park
In comitato Salopiano statuendas curavit

Lindsay Bury
Anno domini MCMLXXXXIV

Those with a classical education should have no trouble with this—and the date!

Finally, for the hall Louisa Kennedy, Tom's wife, made four beautiful plaster reliefs of a substantial size, again commemorating scenes of classical antiquity: *Diana being surprised by Acteon* and *Narcissus looking at his image in a Lake,* being but two of them. As a result of all this activity, the main reception rooms at Millichope now look magnificent, and Sarah and I were very pleased that we had not only been able to restore the house but to furnish it in style. In addition to entertaining our friends, we began a series of concerts in the music room, featuring some wonderful musicians, who have also become good friends. The house was open for a lot of charitable events and over the years there have been many parties.

So, after all the difficult years, Millichope became a happy house and I'm pleased to say it still is.

Chapter Fifteen
Sale of ACT – Going Plural

After the traumatic year of 1986 for ACT, when our dream of seeing Apricot become a major world hardware brand turned to dust, the next step was to repair the finances of the company and look for a way forward. By the interim results of September 1986, we had stabilised the position and the company was back in profit, to the tune of £2,500,000. The first essential step for ACT was to become IBM-compatible. Since we were in the market for supplying business customers, we needed to produce a more upmarket IBM-compatible machine to differentiate ourselves from competitors. The price of personal computers had been falling dramatically, with reductions of up to 50% in the previous six months, fuelled by the flood of cheap IBM clones from the Far East. The personal computer was becoming a commodity. We needed to get out of that business, which we duly did by launching a new upmarket business machine which we called the Zen.

The factory in Scotland, with its 90 employees continued to make computers and workstations and we built quite a significant customer base with the UK government, in its various manifestations. To rebuild the profitability of the company, however, software beckoned as being the least risky and most profitable avenue; ACT Financial Systems, building on its Quasar product, using DEC hardware, was the obvious place to start. Throughout the dramatic years when top management's main attention was focused on first Sirius and then Apricot, our investment banking

Sale of ACT – Going Plural

product, Quasar, had quietly made good progress and was now the most profitable part of the company. Moreover, the overall market for financial systems, and selling to the City, banks, building societies, insurance brokers and others, was growing very fast and a number of other companies had sprung up, exploiting profitable niches in the market. ACT began a programme of acquisitions which, on the whole, were well considered and successful.

The most important development, however, was the disposal of the entire hardware division, which took place in April 1990. Events had been continually pointing that way and getting out of hardware was becoming essential for the company. Competition was remorseless, with the lower end IBM-compatibles selling at commodity-level pricing while further up market, becoming a major vendor to business required levels of financing and commitment that, as a board, we were reluctant to provide. We now prepared in earnest for the sale of Apricot, setting up a data room and appointing two merchant banks to seek a buyer, one for the Far East and the other in the USA. We had had approaches, notably from Siemens and Olivetti. I remember a visit with Roger to Olivetti's headquarters at Ivrea, just outside Turin, where we were introduced to the boss, Carlo de Bennedetti, and his sidekick, Elserino Piol. We spent all of five minutes with de Bennedetti, during which he was on the phone for four and a half; no great meeting of minds there. Neither of these approaches came to anything.

Six more of the world's leading IT companies then expressed interest; most dropped out quickly but negotiations continued with one company, Intel, the world's largest manufacturer of central processors, who were interested in acquiring the manufacturing and design activities of the company. Mitsubishi from Japan also entered the scene showing strong interest. Before long, negotiations came to a head. Michael Hart, our new managing director, was dispatched to London to negotiate with Mitsubishi, while Roger remained in Birmingham, negotiating with Intel, from whom we received an offer letter in April 1990, signed by Andy Grove, no less, their CEO, to buy Apricot for £26 million. It was an extremely difficult balancing act to maintain credible negotiations with two major world companies simultaneously. At one point, Mitsubishi smelt a rat and told Hart they felt they were being strung along under false pretences. By the end of the second day, it was clear that Intel were not going to close, and Foster asked Hart to invite the Japanese to Birmingham where negotiations continued. Meanwhile, we had to disclose to Mitsubishi that the latest profit figures for the hardware division were not good. They had been expecting a profit of £1 million for February and, in the event, there was no profit at all. Finally, a price was agreed of £39 million and the sale was announced on 11th April 1990. Incredibly, this took place within 24 hours of a television programme featuring ACT, where Sir John Harvey Jones, the ex-chief of ICI, turned television-trouble-shooter, advised us to get rid of our hardware division. It must have seemed to the ordinary viewer that the company had taken his advice and done it within 24 hours!

This sale was a remarkable deal for the company; we had a turnover of about £100 million, net assets of about

Sale of ACT – Going Plural

£40 million, and no profits with losses in prospect. To get £39 million in cash looked a good deal in 1990; by the summer of 1992, it seemed miraculous.

From then on, ACT became a fairly conventional software company which grew substantially, largely through good acquisitions in the financial sector. The British software company, BIS was the biggest of these, costing some £90 million and that was a successful buy. The most remarkable, however, was a company in Ireland founded in 1979, called Kindle, which we bought in 1991. They had a product called Bankmaster, which was marketed almost exclusively in Third World countries. An astonishing number of banks in Asia, Africa, Latin America and the Middle East had Bankmaster software; it was robust, well designed and well supported. The two principal architects of the company, Tony Kilduff and Kieran Nagel, had done an amazing job in identifying a relatively neglected area of world banking software; it was a major coup for Roger to have bought both of these companies. In due course, several other infilling acquisitions took place and, by the mid 90s, ACT was one of Europe's leading financial software companies, with profits reaching £28.5 million for the year to March 1994.

By now, we had a different Board of Directors. I had stepped down as chairman in 1989, partly because I had been doing it for 18 years and, secondly, I no longer felt that I had the depth of knowledge of the software industry that the job required, particularly in defining strategy and evaluating acquisitions. Equally important, however, was that we were receiving some pressure from the City to broaden the management bandwidth in the company. Mike Hart had been recruited from Nixdorf and became managing director, and I made way for Roger to become chairman, while I remained a director. A number of other non-executive appointments were made, notably Tony Solomons, my old boss at Singer and Friedlander, who had begun to take an interest in the computer business and had bought a significant shareholding in ACT. I stayed on the board as a non-executive director until ACT's eventual sale in 1995.

The final sale of ACT took place in a hurry. Mismanagement in the financial systems division, which reported to Mike Hart, resulted in a sharp fall in profits, requiring the company to issue a profit warning to the Stock Exchange. Misys, a competitor who had been tracking ACT for quite a while, decided to pounce and launched a successful offer. They made an offer on a Friday afternoon and a price was agreed, together with a commitment to announce to the market on Monday morning. For the next forty eight hours lawyers worked to complete everything in time for the Monday announcement, except apparently one partner of Slaughter and May, who insisted on watching Arsenal on the Saturday afternoon. Sarah and I at the time were on holiday in India, and I was not contactable; phone links were fairly primitive where we were travelling. I was consequently unable to sign any of the documents or, indeed, participate in the discussions, let alone the decision attending the final sale. The offer document recorded a bit of City history because it was sent out by Baring Brothers (in Administration). Barings

Sale of ACT – Going Plural

had just gone bust and they were our advisers! The offer also throughout all the documents referred to *'The directors with the exception of Lindsay Bury unanimously recommend acceptance'*. This attracted the interest of the *Daily Telegraph*, who having enquired about my whereabouts, commented on my absence saying:

> *'Lindsay Bury was travelling in the Himalayas but nobody knew which peak the Old Etonian was attempting to climb.'*

We were in fact in Rajasthan, and nowhere near the Himalayas, but the journalists did manage to find out where I was at school!

It was a sad day for ACT to go out on this note but there was this moment of comic relief at the end. We sold out for £220 million and if shareholders hung onto their Misys shares for a few months, the value more than doubled from that level. So the end result was respectable, although well down from the heady days of 1984.

Well before the sale of ACT, my own career had begun to take a different turn. For some time I had been a non-executive director of several other companies. The most important of these was Portals Holdings, the world's leading manufacturer of mould made banknote paper. I was invited to join the board many years back in 1973, by John Sheffield, who features earlier in this story when I left Eton. His son, Julian, one of my oldest friends since school and Cambridge, became chairman in 1979, and I served on the board as a non-executive director for a remarkable 23 years.

Portals had an interesting history. Founded by Henri

A Shaky Start and a Lot of Luck

Portal, a French Huguenot, in about 1712, the company set up in business in Hampshire and built Overton Mill on the upper reaches of the River Test. An early customer was the Bank of England, and I attended a dinner given by the bank to commemorate the 250th anniversary of the first contract awarded by the Bank of England to Portals for the manufacture of their banknotes. It was a magnificent affair at the Stationers' Hall with the entire court of the Bank present; the table plan records that I was seated next to Kim Cobbold, a former governor who helped me get my first job at Schroders. Both Gordon Richardson, the current governor, and John Sheffield rose to the occasion and spoke impressively.

Partly to ensure a reliable supply of clean water, the Portal family had acquired a beautiful estate on the River Test between Whitchurch and Basingstoke in Hampshire. An agreeable accompaniment to having a secure water supply was some first-class wild brown trout fishing, and a magnificent partridge shoot. In my early years on the Portals board, the Bank of England held about one-third of the shares in the company, and the bank-appointed director, together with one or two other directors and some principal customers, much enjoyed participating in some wonderful days' shooting on the rolling countryside round Laverstoke and Overton. After John Sheffield gave way to Julian as chairman, the company continued to go from strength to strength; throughout my time on the board, I do not think that Portals ever suffered a reversal in profits. The papermaking side was the world leader, benefitting from the Bank of England's custom, and from

Sale of ACT – Going Plural

a large number of overseas central banks, of which the most important was India. This was the mainstay of the business. There was also a water treatment division comprising a number of different businesses, which had been acquired over the years. These were less profitable and more risky, but the overall growth and profitability of Portals Holdings remained remarkably consistent.

In 1989, however, decisive changes took place. The water treatment division was sold to Thames Water for £34 million and Portals made an acquisition in March 1990 of JR Crompton, which took us into the business of the manufacture of specialist, lightweight long fibre papers, particularly used in the manufacture of teabags. The machine to manufacture the teabags cost roughly the same as the proceeds from the sale of water treatment, £35 million! More significantly, however, the Bank of England, who ever since I had been on the board had owned about 32% of the shares in Portals, suddenly decided that they no longer needed to be a shareholder in their supplier, and their entire holding was placed with institutions. This effectively put the company in play; such a consistently profitable and well-managed company with a worldwide spread of blue-chip customers was bound to attract predators, and so it transpired. De La Rue, another of our major customers, who were printers of banknotes as well as many other security-based systems and products, decided that the most valuable security features in banknotes lay in the paper, rather than the printing, and they made an offer which valued the company at about £750 million. It seemed a huge price, and Warburgs our merchant bank, advised us that to reject it would be a difficult decision to justify. So we sold; in many ways a sad day, but a wonderful result for our shareholders.

The central hall at Millichope with Kennedy's masterpiece overhead

This is the Zuloaga parcel gilt chest.
The sale proceeds funded every purchase I made in the house

Starting with the Lion.
Cost £250 to buy and £275 to transport
from Sothebys to Shropshire

Party time in the hall

Mike Stoddart on holiday on the Amazon

Brother-in-law Micky Ingall of Dunbar and Rathbones

Richard Harpin, founder of Homeserve and entrepreneur of genius

David Backhouse. A safe pair of hands with the depositors' money!

Lunch party beneath the pillars, overlooking the lake

Roger Gabb, Johnny Stephens, LCNB and David Scott – a regular Monday four for thirty years. Some great competitive tussles, followed by vodka cocktails from David

Christopher Bland, Amanda Cairns, Sarah and me. I need a new jersey!

Fancy dress party at Millichope. Recently acquired outfits from India. I had to advertise for someone to tie my turban!

Party time again

Frank and Tonie.; engagement shot

Harriet with proud Dad

With Nicholas and Raquel Locke from REGUA near Rio de Janeiro.
The mountain range runs North East from the city

Ian Prance, with three-toed sloth

Mark Rose; a twenty year partnership at Fauna and Flora International.

View from our bedroom at the lodge at REGUA

Right Jura – Loch Tarbert and the Paps Orwell wrote '1984' on Jura

Below Craig Rozga with Mick, glassing the hill for a stag, looking South towards Islay

Jura; stags against raised beach with Loch Tarbert in the background

Sarah's 70th birthday trip to France.

With Frank and Toni, Harriet and Marsha, Willa, Lucas, Albert, Florence, Nell, Isadora and Joy

Chapter Sixteen
The Island of Jura

During the eighties and nineties, while I tussled with the variable fortunes of ACT, our children were growing up and Sarah and I used to take them on holidays, sometimes to the beach with Annette in Spain, or with my sister and her family skiing in the winter. Summer holidays were spent partly at Corsock, Sarah's family home in Scotland, with occasional visits to Horsey Island. Scotland, being Sarah's childhood home was always a lure for her, and after her parents died we used to stay with her elder brother, Micky. By the time the children had reached their teens, Scotland became our favourite destination. We all loved it and it seemed to me that the mixture of exercise, magnificent scenery and a good variety of things to do made Scotland very attractive for a teenage family. We decided to look around to see if a modest property might be for sale, with a range of sporting activities, but without costing too much money or, indeed, involving too much responsibility. We wanted time spent there to be a holiday, not another headache. Sarah and I agreed that an island would be ideal because the sea would provide an additional range of things to do. So we started looking. Our search took us first up to South Uist in the Outer Hebrides, to inspect the island of Rona, which someone told us could be for sale. This seemed a completely desolate place, featuring nothing but flat, boggy landscape, with midges attacking from all directions; there was a solitary house owned by an Italian lady who hadn't been there for some

The Island of Jura

years. When we walked into the living room, the table had not been cleared from their lunch which had probably been eaten two or three years before; flies were buzzing and dust gathering. We decided not to buy.

My friend, Humphry Wakefield (who has already popped up in this narrative!) got to hear of our interest in buying somewhere in Scotland. He was also a friend of William Astor, who owned a very large estate on the island of Jura. In fact, in the 1920s the Astors had bought most of the island from the Campbell family; Nancy Astor, the MP, had sold off the Ardlussa Estate in the north of the island, and now William wanted to sell a further 20,000 acres. My first reaction was that this was far too large, with too much responsibility; I already owned a handsome estate in Shropshire. Why would I want another one? William, however, was having a frustrating time finding a buyer. There was interest from a Frenchman, but when he came to view the mist was down; he could see nothing and the trip was abortive. This was followed by an offer from a game farmer from Norfolk, Andrew Whitham, but after protracted negotiations, he failed to complete. Apparently, he needed to borrow most of the money from an aunt who didn't come up with the wherewithal. Meanwhile, Humphry continued to tell me what a wonderful place it was and that I must go and see it; Rupert Galliers Pratt, whom I had known since Dunbar days, was another good friend of William's and he urged me to go and have a look.

So, finally in October 1984 Sarah and I took a flight from Birmingham to Glasgow, then another flight in a very small plane to the island of Islay. From the airport we then took a taxi to Port Askaig, from where an old wartime landing craft, converted into a ferry, took us across the 800 yard Sound of Islay to the island of Jura. We were met by William, who took us to his home, Tarbert Lodge, about fifteen miles from the ferry, where we arrived for dinner with a view to spending the next day looking at the estate. Early-morning tea was served by a striking dark-haired girl called Heather Petrie who, with her husband, Ian, later came to work for us.

We were then taken down Loch Tarbert, the main sea loch on the southern boundary of the estate, in a large clinker built open boat called *The Crusoe*. That trip of about eight miles was breathtaking; the scenery was wild and magnificent. Although the wind was strong and there was a heavy swell in the outer loch, *The Crusoe's* canvas awning protected us from getting utterly soaked by the waves breaking over the boat, and we had a clear view of grey seals sprawled on rocks, with stags posturing on high ridges, roaring to their hinds, and a golden eagle circling overhead. It was magic. That one trip made up our minds and we came back determined to make an offer. William and I met in my office at Dunbar a week or two later. My offer was quite straightforward; I would take over the Andrew Witham deal on which he had failed to complete. This meant that I wouldn't take over the large Victorian lodge, which looked like a liability, nor several of the fields round the Lodge, together with the farm buildings. Agreement was reached and the price was set at £550,000 for the estate, or roughly £25 per acre.

Ruantallain Estate, as we call it, is one of the remotest and most inaccessible places in Britain. Although only one

The Island of Jura

hundred miles due west of Glasgow, Jura, with the exception of a small pocket of land in the south-east corner, has extremely poor soil, incapable of supporting anything but the most rudimentary agriculture. George Orwell, when he came to Jura to write his novel *1984*, confided to his diary that there were far too many deer, and wrote that the soil ought to be growing something productive. However, the deer predominate for good reason; few other mammals can survive there in the wild. By comparison, with the deer population of about 5,000 animals, the human population is now about 190 on the whole island, although at the time of the herring fishery many years earlier, it was nearer 1,000.

The island is shaped like a lozenge. It is about thirty miles long, stretching from the Sound of Islay in the south, which separates Jura from Islay, to the island of Scarba in the north, from which it is divided by the fearsome whirlpool of the Corryvreckan, apparently classed by the Admiralty as unnavigable in certain weather conditions. Halfway down the island a sea loch nearly splits the island in half, except for a small isthmus, or Tarbert (the name means somewhere across which you can drag a boat from water to water), upon which our house stands. The sea loch, Loch Tarbert, is nearly two miles wide at the west end and from the point of Ruantallain, (which means salt spray rock in Gaelic) at the western extremity of the northern shore of Loch Tarbert, our estate stretches up the Atlantic Coast for six miles. This coastline must be one of the remotest places in Scotland; there is not a single road or even track which goes out there, and the shoreline is rocky and dangerous for most vessels. It is listed as one of thirty Wild Places in Scotland in the Scottish National Heritage classification. The entire coastline on the northern shore of Loch Tarbert and the whole of the western shoreline of Jura is an SSSI (Sire of Special Scientific Interest), featuring the raised beaches, completely protected from any human activity and almost inaccessible except by boat. Whereas the walking on the east side of the island is very tough, involving much tussocky, molinia grass which deters almost all walkers, the west coast is drier with more heather and machair type vegetation; the walking there is very good, with spectacular scenery. It is an utterly remote shoreline with only deer, seals, the occasional otter and some feral goats, which legend has it came over from the wreckage of the Spanish Armada in the 16th century. Overhead, there is no shortage of avian predators; apart from the usual gulls, golden and sea eagles, peregrine falcons, hen harriers and merlins are regularly to be seen.

Everywhere, the views are magnificent; looking south across outer Loch Tarbert, a huge prospect unfolds, of the Paps of Jura, three substantial mountains, which dominate the southern half of the island. To the west, about twenty miles across the Atlantic, lie the islands of Colonsay and Oronsay, and to the north, the Island of Mull, with the 3,000 foot peak of Ben More clearly visible. There is an abundance of red deer and some first-class wild brown trout fishing. There are at least thirty lochs on Ruantallain estate containing fish, and the large concentration of hinds on the Atlantic coastline draws in the stags during the annual rut in the autumn, with the result that the stag shooting is second to none, with some heavy stags; beasts up to 17 or 18 stone are by no means uncommon. It is a paradise and, even now, thirty-five years, later I cannot believe my good fortune in having been able to buy it.

Although, by taking over the Witham deal, in my negotiations with William Astor, I'd avoided buying anything except a wooden bungalow complex built by William's uncle, David Astor, together with a couple of cottages, a considerable amount of money needed to be spent. It is thought that all estates on the west coast of Scotland lose money, and Ruantallain is certainly no exception. Why the Scottish National Party should want to change the current arrangements whereby landlords, mainly non-Scottish, pour money into these remote highland estates, providing jobs and bringing opportunities for the local communities, is a mystery to me. In addition to completely renovating the house, I had to buy a seaworthy boat capable of conveying friends and paying guests across some very rough seas. Rifles, fishing rods, hill machines capable of climbing very steep mountains, together with many other items had to be acquired.

The capital outlay was only part of the story; we also needed to employ people. A stalker and a ghillie, a cook and housekeeper were the essential minimum. And this was supposed to be a relaxing holiday home without responsibilities! It was all a long way from our original quest.

Finally, there was the need to earn some revenue. I couldn't possibly afford to employ all these people without having any money coming in. Letting the stalking during the short season in the autumn was essential and after several years I have managed to build up a good list of sporting tenants, most of whom come back every year. All this has consumed a considerable amount of time and money. Over the thirty-four years I have owned the estate, I have had the good fortune to employ three outstanding stalkers: Iain Petrie, John Connor and Craig Rozga, who is still with me; Peter Campbell from Ardlussa, the estate immediately to the north, also joined us for seven years until his recent death. Together with Heather Petrie, Annette Campbell, and our two outstanding cooks, Ros Cooper and Fran Orio, we have built up a wonderful team, and their support and enthusiasm over so many years have made our time in the Highlands tremendously enjoyable, and I like to think we have also brought some benefits to the island.

An amusing episode took place one November when Linda Collins my secretary in Birmingham who helped with the Jura bookkeeping, buttonholed me.

'Lindsay, I think the game dealers are cheating you,' she said. 'They've stopped paying you for the pizzles.'

The pizzles are, in fact, the stags' penis and testicles, and highly esteemed by Japanese consumers. I had to explain that stag shooting finished at the end of October and in November the female deer, called hinds, were the target and, being female, they didn't have any pizzles. Linda was relieved to hear this.

Sarah has established a charming garden on Jura just behind the house, which first of all required fencing off the deer, which had formerly had the run of the garden, and became used to peering through the windows of the

The Island of Jura

house. It has been very tough going, because trees and shrubs hate the gales which sweep across the island often at force eight or nine, enough to uproot big trees. It has been a long process of trial and error to see what will grow but now after more than thirty years some beautiful shrubs and flowers have become well established and enhance the natural contours of rocks and streams, which were already there. I have also created (with generous help from the Scottish taxpayer) about seven native hardwood plantations on the east side of the estate, totalling about 250 acres. On the whole, with one exception, these have grown well, and they are now beginning to look like woods, as opposed to plantations. The gales greatly limit the sites where it is possible to plant, but by now most of the woods are reasonably well established.

This has all demanded considerable effort from Sarah and me. I don't employ an agent and do all the letting myself, which is quite a chore, but I have managed to build up a good base of tenants, not only for stalking but also for fishing in the spring. Some regulars come every year - most notably Robert Pryor, an old Cambridge friend and a judge, who is a passionate fisherman and chairman of the prestigious Houghton Club, on the River Test in Hampshire. Robert came over from a week's fishing on the Spey to stay with us for a few days in 1985 and since then has taken a week, sometimes a fortnight, for the last thirty years. It was surprising to me that such a distinguished fisherman, together with Virginia his wife, who is also highly accomplished, could spend so much time pursuing our very small trout, but they have done just that for all those years and they still do.

Now that I am retired and Frank runs Millichope Estate, Sarah and I still run Ruantallain in conjunction with our daughter Harriet, who now owns it. One of my chief pleasures these days is to spend time with the many friends we have made on the island. We have got to know some wonderful characters, and have absolutely not encountered any of the animosity towards the English that we were told is so widespread, and we feel very much at home on Jura.

One of the great annual events on Jura is the Fell Race, which is seventeen miles long and involves climbing up and down seven hills, including the three Paps of Jura, which rise from sea level to two thousand seven hundred feet very steeply. The record winning time, which was achieved this year, is three hours five minutes, and most of the contestants are from well-known running clubs in the Highlands, as well as the Lake District and Yorkshire. I was incredibly proud of my son Frank, then aged forty-six, who entered and came 151st out of 270 entrants, doing it in five hours fifteen minutes, the best time achieved by anyone from the island in that year.

The purchase of Jura was a life-changing event for me and one of my main enthusiasms, as I get old, is to put something back into the island which has given us so many happy memories.

Chapter Seventeen
Sharp Technology and Venture Capital

After the sale of Dunbar in 1984, and ACT in 1995, I found myself without a full-time job. It would have been easy at this stage to settle down and run my two magnificent estates, Millichope and Ruantallain. However, I love business and although the shares in ACT had recovered well from their low point in 1986, they had by no means recovered their earlier glory. I was only fifty and was receiving offers. The most interesting of these came from Simon Sharp, senior partner of Albert E Sharp, stockbrokers in Birmingham. Sharps were the leading firm of stockbrokers in the city, and had represented ACT during its career as a public company. In addition to the quoted investment side, Sharps had a subsidiary called Summit, a small venture capital firm run by Nick Talbot Rice and Ran Meinertzhagen. Summit was reasonably successful and Simon suggested that I should head up a third fund specialising in technology. Because of my long career with ACT I was expected to know something about technology. It was to be based in Birmingham with an independent board of directors under Simon as chairman, and it seemed a reasonable idea. I agreed and £10 million was raised with a member of the Summit team, Casper Weston, seconded to me, and we started in business as the Sharp Technology Fund.

Unfortunately, it turned out to be a poorly-conceived venture and over its ten years of life only achieved very moderate returns. There were a number of problems. First,

Sharp Technology and Venture Capital

I had very little knowledge about the venture capital business, the structuring of deals, the finding of good companies to back and establishing the network of contacts, essential to help in locating them. Sharp's background was mainly in Birmingham-based companies, which meant manufacturing and engineering, not technology, and Birmingham was not the best place to be for a high-tech fund, particularly compared with London or Cambridge. Above all, I hadn't realised that very early-stage technology investment was an extremely difficult area of the market to make money. Apart from all the usual risks which attend any early-stage investment, these companies rarely achieve a decent cash flow, making borrowing or leveraged capital structures impossible. Even if successful, the UK is not a viable market on its own; technology by its very nature has to be international and become established on world markets. As ACT had found, entering the US, in particular, is fraught with pitfalls.

Nevertheless, we did find some good companies and the whole exercise was interesting. Our most successful was called Microprocessor and Memory Distribution, based in Reading, and this was a co-investment with Schroder Ventures (later to become Permira), where I had joined the board as a non-executive director at its formation. Through this I had got to know Jon Moulton and Peter Smitham, who were both outstandingly successful in the private equity business. Some of the investments went wrong; notably a company based in Leicester called Marwin, which was the brainchild of a visionary engineer, Ernest Hopwell. The company made enormous metal profiling machines,

A Shaky Start and a Lot of Luck

exclusively for British Aerospace; one of these, for which we charged £3 million, was used to make the wings of the Airbus. Sadly, the company was too dependent on a handful of very large orders from one customer, and repeatedly had to raise new capital. There was no profit for us there.

Another business, Sapphire Holdings, was rather like ACT, in finding an outstanding US product and becoming overwhelmingly the major sales outlet for it in the UK. The product was a software database called DataEase, which became the market leader for an entry-level database on PCs. DataEase was a US company, and relations with them were not good. I remember endless meetings in Trumbull, Connecticut, in the US, during which we wrangled with the board of Dataease as to which company was going to take over the other. In the event, despite establishing Dataease as one of the leading small company databases in Britain, we were unsuccessful in making any money out of the investment.

On the subject of Sapphire, I had a most traumatic experience while staying in the Bear Hotel in Woodstock, near Blenheim. I was with Stephen Page, the CEO, and we were entertaining a prospective Japanese client. We had a dinner at which quite a lot of alcohol was consumed following which, quite late, we went to our rooms. Mine was in an annexe called the Tudor Suite. In the middle of the night, I needed to go to the bathroom but the door was identical to the door out into the passage. In my befuddled state, I made an extremely bad choice and found myself in the passage completely naked, with my bedroom door locked. Not a happy predicament! I walked across the

Sharp Technology and Venture Capital

gravel to reception in the main hotel but there was not a soul about. After a quick visit to the dining room which was laid up for breakfast, I removed a table cloth from one of the tables to cover myself and returned to the lobby. Eventually, after tiptoeing across the gravel from reception to the Tudor suite and back, fruitlessly trying many keys, I noticed that the key to room 21 was still hanging on the rack, while the computer showed that room 21 was vacant. It was worth a try and so I removed the key and eventually found room 21, which was, indeed, vacant. The immediate problem was solved, although I didn't sleep very well and the following morning I had to ring reception and ask if room service would bring all my clothes, toothbrush, razor and other accessories from the Tudor Suite to room 21.

I can't remember whether Sapphire got charged for both rooms, or whether the Japanese client gave us any additional business!

Almost our final investment was to participate in a rescue fundraising in Shire Pharmaceuticals, one of the big success stories of the London Stock Exchange in recent years. It was an existing portfolio investment by Schroder Ventures, and we invested in parallel with them in November 2002; the company was due to run out of money by March. However, it went public in February, raising plenty of cash and our loan was repaid on handsome terms. If we had hung on and switched to the equity, Sharp Technology would have made its shareholders a great deal of money and the final IRR of the fund would have been transformed. As it was, the figure during the whole lifetime of Sharp Technology was 5%. Not great!

A Shaky Start and a Lot of Luck

Sharp Technology, although good fun, was not rewarding financially but in 1992 I was asked by Sharps to take over the management of Summit. Ran Meinertzhagen had by then retired, and Nick Talbot Rice and I were joined by David Sankey. Schroder Ventures, with whom I had by then established a good relationship, had expressed an interest in taking a shareholding in the management company of Summit, and I also took a direct equity stake. The timing was perfect; there had been a stock market crash in 1995 and the shares in Summit, which was listed in 1986 as a quoted company, were standing at a fraction of the market capitalisation. The companies in the portfolio were unexciting run-of-the-mill enterprises, but solidly based, and it was just a question of gradually selling them off and watching the share price rise.

Along with Schroder Ventures, I bought a share in the management company as well as a sizeable shareholding in Summit shares. Summit in due course liquidated (it had a termination date of 1997), and the management company was sold to Murray Johnstone. It was a profitable, if small scale exercise for Schroder Ventures, but much more significant for myself. Schroder Ventures put out a statement:

'You may have read in the press that we have sold our stake in Summit Equity Ventures to Murray Johnstone Private Equity. Our original relationship with Summit was established in 1992, in partnership with Albert E Sharp, North of England ventures and Lindsay Bury. Our involvement with Summit was mutually beneficial; the share price of Summit plc rose

from 50p per share to £1.85 per share over the period of our investment.

We wish Lindsay Bury, David Sankey and the rest of the team of Summit every success in their new partnership with Murray Johnstone Private Equity.'

The sale of Summit to Murray Johnstone was very profitable for me, because I not only controlled the management and was in a good position to know the underlying value of the portfolio companies, but the market, in its wisdom, had chosen to mark the shares down to 20% of asset value. I bought a lot of shares in Summit and also did well on the sale of the management company to Murray Johnstone. So although Sharp Technology was a slog for very little return, Summit was a different story altogether. I got a nice letter from Peter Smitham, who shortly afterwards became chief executive of Permira:

Dear Lindsay

Thank you very much for firstly, allowing Schroder Ventures to be involved with you in buying Summit; secondly, for all the fun we had working with you and how successful it has been; thirdly, for having the foresight (cheek!) to ask MJ for such a price.

Lindsay, it has been a fun and profitable relationship. Thank you and best wishes.

Yours sincerely, Peter Smitham

Chapter Eighteen
Bonanza –
South Staffordshire Water

In 1992 I accepted what seemed a strange invitation. Teddy Thompson, a director of Wolverhampton and Dudley Breweries, whom I knew socially in Shropshire, came to see me in my office and asked whether I might be interested in becoming a director of the South Staffordshire Water Company (SSWC). This was a statutory water company whose sole activity was to supply water to a strange-shaped sliver of country in the county of Staffordshire, running from Tipton in the Black Country, bypassing Wolverhampton, and continuing up via Lichfield and Burton on Trent, to Uttoxeter and Ashbourne in Derbyshire. The head office was in Sheepcote Street, in the middle of Birmingham, only a few hundred yards from ACT's offices. I really couldn't see any reason to take this on; the non-executives had nothing to do except make sure the water supply continued uninterrupted, and the water rates were sent out and payment collected. I dithered, and then finally decided to say yes, mainly because the board meetings were so close and wouldn't take much time. The real clincher, however, was that we got our cars beautifully cleaned during each meeting; I also discovered that the lunches were good and the other directors congenial. The board consisted of a number of prominent local businessmen, with several from Tarmac. Apart from Teddy, there was Sir Charles Burman, chairman, Geoff Wright, Vernon Lancaster and an engineer called Jack Thompson, the father of Annie Gabb, and a great friend. It was all very cosy and we received modest fees for a modest amount of work.

All this suddenly changed in 1989, when Margaret Thatcher decided to privatise the water industry. Teddy Thompson had meanwhile succeeded Charles Burman as the chairman of SSWC, and before long Teddy came up to retirement age and the board invited me to succeed him as chairman. I therefore was to preside over the birth of SSWC as a listed company. This took place in 1993. The company was recapitalized, with the old preference share structure giving way to a mix of preference and ordinary shares. At the same time, Compagnie Generale des Eaux, the largest water company in France, were buying shares in several of the privatised water companies and before long they had built up a holding of 30% in our shares. The French didn't appoint a director, but the executive in charge of our holding was an amiable chap who came from Oran in Algeria, called Jean Claude Banon. We were free to appoint our own board and many of the new appointees were friends of mine in business, working in the Midlands: Hugh Meynell, Panton Corbett, Simon Kenyon Slaney and David Sankey were four of them.

I soon found that South Staffordshire was a very well-run company, and that the day-to-day operations could safely be left to the first-class, and highly professional management. We had good relationships with leaders in the industry, notably Ian Byatt the head of OFWAT, and the directors of Seven Trent Water Company, on whose behalf we collected the sewerage charges due to them from

A Shaky Start and a Lot of Luck

our customers. South Staffs was only a water company, and the sewerage treatment to our customers was supplied by Severn Trent. We also undertook various contracting activities in overseas countries, notably Nepal and Malawi, and every two years we took part in a World Water Industry Conference, which was held in some agreeable cities dotted round the world. I remember, in 1995 there was one such conference in Durban, South Africa. We decided to entertain our principal African customer to a dinner. His name was Tikani Banda, presumably a relative of Dr Hastings Banda, the head of state in Malawi. Tikani was in charge of the Malawi Water Company, and we were putting in a billing system for them. We duly chose a good restaurant, as befits a good customer, and on the appointed evening awaited his arrival. I was astonished to see ten guests arrive, as opposed to the two we had been expecting, nearly all of them very large women. It was explained that they were important executives in his company. We inspected the menu. I asked Tikani if he would like lobster.

'Yeees, please,' he replied.

'And your friends. What would they like?'

'They all very fond of lobster.'

Dinner duly took place, and the large squad of women never looked up from their plates, shovelling in their lobsters in complete silence. At the end of dinner, I asked Tikani if he would like a brandy.

'Yees, please.'

'And your friends?'

'They all very fond of brandy.'

Brandy was duly served, several bottles of it. Finally

Bonanza – South Staffordshire Water

I asked whether everything was all right and relations between the two companies were as they should be.

'Well, yees, but I see South Staffs shares go up every week – very good shares. Would there be any chance of some friendship shares?'

This was too much; the dinner had already cost a fortune and the limit been reached. If precedent was anything to go by, I would have had to shell out friendship shares to all the women too!

'Well, Tikani, we have ordinary shares and preference shares, but we don't have any friendship shares, so I'm afraid what you request is impossible.'

It was a good try.

Two significant developments took place in the industry at the time of privatisation. First, we were allowed to diversify. Many of the leading companies in the industry, the big water companies, started making substantial, and in many cases, unwise takeovers. At the same time, the directors greatly increased their own salaries. South Staffs were in a strong position because our water rates were the lowest in the industry. We were also in the enviable position of having very low charges and satisfactory profitability. We appointed a new chief executive, John Harris, with whom I established a close working relationship and the following years were most enjoyable and profitable for the company. John was keen to make diversifications by acquiring little businesses and we looked at countless proposals, both within and outside the water industry. I was wary, but took the view that it was unrealistic to object to them all. I tried to ensure that they were all pretty

A Shaky Start and a Lot of Luck

small and we made quite a few minor acquisitions, which didn't do particularly well or particularly badly.

In due course, however, we found a once-in-a-lifetime opportunity. A young accountant from Newcastle on Tyne, called Richard Harpin, came to see us with an idea to set up a plumbing franchise as a joint venture with a water company. I don't like franchising and was quite sceptical, but there was a major shortage of plumbers in the country, and Richard saw that a competitive advantage was to be obtained by selling plumbing through a water company. He had already tried several other water companies and we were the first to show interest.

We decided to go for it and bought 51% of the company, which was then called Fastfix, for £100,000. We also had an option to increase our shareholding to 75%, using a pricing formula of 4PE. We jointly set a budget for Fastfix, which contained the usual wildly optimistic forecasts with sales and profit projections rising steadily from South East to North West on the graph. These projections are almost never believed. Homeserve (the new name for Fastfix) was different; a profit of £1 million was forecast within five years; in fact they made £7 million!

Before long, the idea had broadened from just providing plumbing to selling insurance. Richard had created an insurance policy to sell to homeowners, to protect them from the risks of pipes bursting or leaking, specifically the pipe between the mains water pipe running down the street, which connected to the point where it entered the policyholder's house. Apparently the incidence of bursts is quite high, and Richard saw an opportunity.

Bonanza – South Staffordshire Water

Richard's idea was to sell an insurance policy through the water companies, starting with South Staffs, and then broadening it out to the whole industry. A trial mailing of 1,000 leaflets was sent out to South Staffs' customers, and the take-up was 3.8%. This was considered an excellent result. Most of our big mail shots over the next five years had take-up rates of just over 1%, although there were exceptions like Guildford in Surrey, where there was an acute shortage of plumbers, with a take-up rate of 13%. Rates of just over 1% were the norm. The cost of the policy was £39.95, and this first South Staffs mailing brought in thirty-eight customers. That yielded £1,482 of revenue. That was on one very small mail shot, but from that moment Richard was convinced he was on to a winner. Of the £39.95 price charged for the policy, underwriting the risk cost about £15 and about 10% went to the water company, whose name appeared on the circular, leaving a very handsome margin for Homeserve. All we, at South Staffs and the other water companies had to do, was to put our name on the leaflet; all claims coming in went to Homeserve who then sent out plumbers from their network to attend to the repair. Indeed, Homeserve were also responsible for the mail shots, where the creative artwork and copy was down to them, although it had of course to be approved by the relevant water company. It has become known as affinity marketing.

Having exhausted the potential of South Staffordshire customers, the major challenge was to persuade the big water utilities to take it up. This took about three years and involved a huge effort by Richard and his team;

A Shaky Start and a Lot of Luck

Richard was young and so was his company; South Staffs were a competitor to the other companies, who were highly conservative and worried about the risk to their reputation; above all the reaction was, 'Not invented here. We can do this ourselves.' These numerous and understandable reservations were finally only overcome by evidence of good trading by their rivals, who were making useful effort-free money by using Homeserve. A major breakthrough took place, when Anglian Water decided to adopt the policy and volumes rose enormously. Within three years, Homeserve succeeded in capturing the whole country, and the number of policies sold per annum was about three million. The retention rate was about 90% and about 75% of these paid by direct debit.

We were all amused at one of our monthly board meetings, when a member of the staff came up with a tray upon which was a letter addressed to me. In it was one of our circulars to an Anglian Water customer, which had been returned from a Cambridge postal district. A note had been scrawled on it in a felt tipped pen with elegant handwriting.

'Fuck off. May the fleas from a thousand camels infest your chairman's arsehole.'

This caused a good deal of merriment at our board meeting, and since then it has hung in the gent's lavatory at Millichope, where it causes general amusement.

After five years' trading, Homeserve was making a profit of an incredible £7 million a year and we had exercised our option to increase our shareholding to 75%. The rest of the shares were held by Richard and a friend from Newcastle,

Bonanza – South Staffordshire Water

Jeremy Middleton, who had helped him set up the business. Looking further ahead, the profitability of Homeserve was going to exceed the rest of the water company, and Richard was pressing that Homeserve should be spun off as a separate company with its own quotation on the stock market. In due course, we yielded to that pressure. However, instead of listening to the blandishments of the private equity industry, who were all beating at my door, including such distinguished suitors as Christopher Bland from Warburg Pincus, and William Waldegrave from UBS, both of whom wished to acquire South Staffs and spin off Homeserve, we decided to do it ourselves. With the assistance of Cazenove, we drew up a plan whereby our own shareholders would receive direct shares in Homeserve, as well as their existing shares in South Staffs. This way, our own shareholders kept all the upside potential in both companies.

At the time of the split, South Staffs shares were standing about 632p, after a long steady rise. Of the two shares which shareholders received, Homeserve has risen to a price of about £18 a share, at which the company is valued at well over £2 billion, while South Staffs was taken over shortly after at £11.50 per share. It is the most profitable deal with which I have ever been involved. At the time of writing, Homeserve has entered overseas markets and, after the usual careful build-up, has achieved further dramatic success; in the USA they now have £3 million customers.

Looking back on this story, I don't think any of us realised what an astonishing achievement this was:

Richard, in founding and building up a £2 billion company, inventing a completely new route to market for plumbing insurance and John Harris the managing director of SSWC in seeing the potential and making the investment. No other company in the water industry made a significant success of their diversification efforts. Indeed, they received in many cases much abuse from their shareholders, and the press, as well a very jaundiced reception from Ian Byatt, the chief of OFWAT, the industry regulator. Homeserve had few regrets over their deal with us, which gave us 75% of the company. Jeremy Middleton wrote in their company history called *Twenty: the Homeserve Story:*

> 'South Staffs were a very supportive shareholder. Yes we would have liked to have held on to more of the company, but it was a fair deal. Let's just say the most important thing is to grow the cake and not to worry too much about how it is cut.'

My own reign as chairman was very nearly ruined by my support for one highly unsuitable diversification. The proposal was put to us in 2002 to acquire Dowding and Mills, which was an electrical winding company based in Birmingham. Simon Sharp was the chairman, and we shared a non-executive director, David Sankey, who sat on the boards of both Dowding and Mills and SSWC. Superficially, the idea looked attractive; the company was doing badly, but it was a well-established business with good potential for a rebound. I also felt that, with a director on the board, we would be less likely to find any skeletons in the cupboard, which normally emerge after an acquisition. We did, however, encounter opposition from our largest shareholder, Jean Claude Banon, representing Compagnie General des Eaux. He had never liked our diversifications, although the success of Homeserve had somewhat blunted his criticisms, but taking over a fairly sizeable listed company in a completely strange industry was something he would not support. We were advised by Cazenove that it was very unwise to go ahead in the face of opposition from our largest shareholder, and so we dropped the idea. In fact, he did us a huge service; Dowding and Mills went through several years of extremely bad trading and would have been a great drag on our profits. Jean Claude's opposition saved us from making fools of ourselves. Once again, I had been lucky.

Following the split of the company into South Staffordshire and Homeserve, I decided not to be a candidate for chairman of either company. I had been on the board for 23 years and chairman for 13. I felt it was time to move on. Water companies, like other utilities, will always be attractive to private equity, due to the predictable cash flows which enable a capital structure with a good deal of debt and much of the industry is now in the hands of foreign owners or private equity. I think it is a pity, however, that the link between water supply and local shareholders and boards of directors has been decisively broken, but I suppose that is a consequence of privatization, and I of all people can't complain, having done spectacularly well from my shareholding in SSWC.

Chapter Nineteen
Sage and Others

In 1995, just after the sale of ACT, David Goldman, the chairman of the Sage Group requested a meeting with me. He came round to my flat with two colleagues – Michael Jackson, a non-executive director, and Paul Walker, who had just been appointed chief executive. We had met previously at a lunch at Singer and Friedlander. Sage had established an enviable position as market leader in small business accounting systems: this was an area which ACT had also covered, but not with sufficient focus and depth. Sage was now a public company and they were looking around for two non-executive directors; I was asked if I would be interested. The company had been founded by Goldman, who was a printer in Newcastle, together with Graham Wylie, a programmer, and they set up a suite of basic accountancy packages. Goldman was a shrewd and able man; the company was tightly controlled, with aggressive and highly effective marketing, and it achieved exceptional profit margins. The entry-level small business accounting packages, that then accounted for the majority of turnover, enjoyed pre-tax margins of up to 50%.

I went up to Newcastle, met the management, and agreed to join the board. Paul Walker was an inspired choice as chief executive, and he undoubtedly was the architect of the group's remarkable success during the eleven years that I was on the board. Unfortunately, I only overlapped with David for a year, before he gave up the chair through bad health. Michael Jackson then took over, and Sage embarked on a series of overseas acquisitions starting with France, then Germany and Spain and, later, the United States.

Before long, the company's turnover was split roughly one third UK, one third Europe, and one third US. On the face of it, this acquisition spree should have ended in tears. We picked out leading companies in the small business accounting sector in various countries, all of whom were using different software. They were entrepreneurial companies, normally still run by the founder and, typically, with 10,000–20,000 customers, and often not particularly profitable. We would then usually pay for the acquisitions in cash, mostly buying goodwill; on the face of it, a suicidal business model.

The one key factor, however, was the fact that accountancy is a notoriously sticky application, meaning that for a client, changing accountancy systems is a real nuisance and customers are most reluctant to do it, unless they have to. This meant that if you bought a list of customers, generally they stayed with you. After acquisition, we then applied the Sage formula. Nearly always, the acquired company had a core product which was profitable and the financial backbone of the company. Before long, however, the founder gets bored of the core product and invents a new one further upmarket with fancy new bells and whistles. This new product was nearly always draining away the cash and profitability of the company.

Sage's formula was to scrap the new product, go back to a much more thorough and effective exploitation of the standard product, while keeping it up-to-date with relatively minor software upgrades and enhancements. It nearly always worked, and we usually managed to achieve a 20% margin pre-tax on sales within two years on the acquired company. This meant that, within two years, the acquired company would be accumulating cash, which enabled us, in 90% of cases, to pay cash for the acquisition. The result was that Sage's balance sheet often looked awful with substantial short-term indebtedness, but the cash flow was very strong and the company's profits grew strongly. We rarely issued equity.

As it happened, this very rapid growth in profits, resulting mainly from international acquisitions, coincided with a stock market boom in the mid-90s. At the forefront of the boom were so-called technology companies, and this particular bull market became known as the dot-com boom. Sage was a front runner in the technology sector and, at one stage, the market capitalisation of the company equalled that of British American Tobacco – a vastly larger company!

Naturally, I greatly enjoyed being a part of this remarkable success story. I made about six trips a year to Newcastle, a city I came to like very much, and the board also used to have long distance away weekends in agreeable places like Paris, Newport Beach, and Palm Springs California. As usual, I bought quite a few shares in Sage, much enjoyed the rise, and then gnashed my teeth when the ensuing dot-com crash brought the share price right back down again. As a director it is always difficult to sell shares; there is never a right time.

Towards the end of my time at Sage in 2005, I was the

senior non-executive director, and became more centrally involved in the future direction of the company. The chairman, Michael Jackson, had received an offer to become chairman of a company called PartyGaming, which had established a platform to enable online poker to be played and, since it covered the whole of the United States, it was making a great deal of money. The company was run by Indians (Asiatic as opposed to Red), and the largest shareholder was a man called Anurag Dikshit. Michael was to become chairman and get paid a huge salary, with many options and other incentives. He had already accepted and the company had embarked on getting a listing on the London Stock Exchange.

The trouble was that, according to recently-introduced rules on corporate governance, a chairman of a FTSE 100 company such as Sage was not allowed to be chairman of a second, the idea being that one chairmanship was quite enough, and it was not possible or appropriate for a chairman to devote enough time to two major companies simultaneously. Since it was clear that PartyGaming, which was making hundreds of millions of pounds a year, would vault straight into the FTSE 100 index after the flotation, this was going to cause Michael a problem. He would have to choose between Sage and PartyGaming, but he wanted to keep both. Michael's tactics were initially to invite each of the non-executive directors to a one-on-one meeting, explaining the situation and eliciting their views. I was unaware of the new rules and told Michael that I couldn't see a major problem. I very soon realised, however, that this was a big mistake and there would, indeed, be a considerable problem. As the senior non-executive director, it fell to me to deliver the board's response. Michael had already accepted the chairmanship of PartyGaming and, since they were on about proof 10 of the prospectus, it was likely that the company would sue him for a lot of money if he withdrew. The only realistic option was for him to resign from Sage. We had a meeting of the non-executive directors, and it was unanimously agreed that I should communicate this to Michael, which I duly did.

Apart from being in breach of the stock exchange requirements on multiple chairmanships, there would have been a reputational risk to Sage, which was absolutely unacceptable. PartyGaming was based in Gibraltar, a tax haven beyond the reaches of the Internal Revenue Service of the United States. What they were doing was illegal in the US, and could prevent Michael from visiting the US as chairman of Sage. With one third of the company's business in the US, this was less than ideal, to put it mildly.

In many ways, we were sad to lose Michael, who was good company, and had presided over the fastest period of the company's growth, but he had to go and, as senior non-executive, it was my job to lead the search for a successor. I worked closely with Paul Walker and the board. We retained headhunters, Anna Mann and in due course we came up with Julian Horn Smith, the deputy chairman of Vodafone. On paper, this should have been an ideal choice; he had the experience and had seen a technology company through a period of huge growth. I had an extended conversation on the phone with Chris

Sage and Others

Gent, the CEO of Vodafone, who gave Julian a warm endorsement, and we went ahead and made the appointment. However, within a year the non-executive directors of Sage got rid of him.

By this time, I had left Sage, having been on the board for 11 years, and the time had come for me to step down. Six months after I left the board, I read that Julian had resigned. I have heard several versions of what happened. I like to think that if I had remained on, I might have been able to build a bridge between the chairman and the non-executives and, working with Paul, enable Julian to make a success of his chairmanship. However, Julian completely misread Sage, failing to understand the culture of the company; apparently, he did not even chair the board meetings well, and the board decided to ask him to resign.

I left the board in 2006, and have followed Sage's progress ever since. The successor to Paul was Guy Berruyer, a Frenchman, who had been running Sage's European operations. He had a good analytical approach to business and was a safe pair of hands. I kept in touch with him after leaving the company, and am pleased to say that, at the time of writing, Sage is the U.K.'s most valuable technology company, situated halfway up the list of FTSE 100 companies, and capitalised at £8 billion.

During the period when I was travelling up and down to Newcastle on Sage's affairs, I was also a director of two other interesting companies, one in Cambridge and the other in Stafford, both listed on the London Stock Exchange. The Cambridge company was called Roxboro, the name of the town in North Carolina in the US, which

A Shaky Start and a Lot of Luck

was the home of Dialight, its principal subsidiary. Peter Smitham from Schroder Ventures, who had put the company together, had suggested me as a non-executive. It was a good company, resulting from a successful portfolio investment by Schroder Ventures (or Permira as it is now called). The main subsidiary was Dialight, and their business was LED (light emitting diode) arrays. LEDs were, at that stage, mainly to be seen on the consoles of music players and instrument panels, appearing as little dots of light. Dialight's job was to arrange the LEDs into arrays, which would maximise their effectiveness. One of the early major applications has been traffic lights, but appropriate design is required to optimise the display of light for whatever application is chosen.

The LEDs were sourced from Hewlett-Packard and Philips, and we were substantial customers of both companies. Nowadays, LEDs are taking over from incandescent bulbs everywhere. Most traffic lights, airport runway lights, much industrial lighting and, indeed, many domestic lights have been taken over by LEDs. Although they cost more initially than the traditional incandescent bulbs, they give a better targeted light, have a longer life, and use less power. The chief executive and a substantial shareholder was called Harry Tee, a colourful character and, by and large, a successful CEO. He lived in Much Hadham and was an enthusiastic supporter of the Conservative Party.

The non-executives included Peter Curry, the founder of Unitech, and Richard Koch, who lectures on business and has been a highly successful entrepreneur in his own right. Dialight still exists as an independent company listed on the stock exchange, although management has changed. The company started life in Newmarket and then moved to Cambridge. I served on the board of Roxboro for eight years, from 1993 to 2001, and although the company was successful and I enjoyed my time there, I cannot say that I made much of a contribution other than to introduce them to Cazenove, who became our corporate broker.

Another company where I served as chairman for two years was Unicorn International. This was quite unlike anything I'd done before, and was nothing to do with technology or, indeed, finance. It was an old established engineering company, whose main activity was grinding automobile crankshafts and windscreens. I came across it through Jon Moulton, who was working at the time for the venture capital company, Apax, with Ronnie Cohen, the chief executive and founder of Apax UK. Apax had acquired Unicorn and put in a managing director, David Rimmer; the company had done quite well and was going to float as a public company and they needed a chairman. I was quite intrigued and pleased to be involved again in a Midlands company fairly close by, in Staffordshire. Grinding is a dirty business, and the company's main factory is just by Stafford Railway Station. Considering how little money grinding companies all over the world make, the size of the premises and the number of employees required always surprised me. As well as Stafford, there were a number of other UK sites, in addition to subsidiaries in France and Germany. The largest and most profitable subsidiaries were situated in the United States, in Detroit and Chicago, near the big automobile companies. I got on well with David and, indeed, the rest of the board and spent a considerable amount of time visiting subsidiaries, trying to understand what was going on. The company's internal figures were robust enough to support a flotation; I had retained Cazenove and we were on the critical path to go public.

What I did not know is that Jon Moulton, a Unicorn board member, was simultaneously negotiating to sell the company to another major UK engineering group. We discovered this quite late in the proceedings, when we had lined up a number of institutions to take stock on the flotation, and had a firm deadline for the issue. In fact this was a strong position because, had the float been aborted in order to allow negotiations with the third party to proceed, we would have been in a weaker negotiating position with the potential acquirer, because we would have lost our position in the stock exchange queue. Our prospective institutional investors would certainly have taken a dim view, making a listing impossible for several years after. So we did go public, and the shares did reasonably well. After twelve months, we had an approach from Saint Gobain the big French glass conglomerate, who were also world leaders in grinding, having bought Norton in the US. A price was obtained, which showed Apax a good profit and the whole exercise was successful.

I also benefitted indirectly from the sale because Ronnie Cohen then invited me to join a group of investors in one of his VC syndicates, who were able to invest alongside his institutional investors in Apax's target companies, without having to pay a management fee. I was on a couple of these syndicates and they did very well.

In 1995, I resumed my connection with the City by joining the board of Electric and General Investment Trust. Christopher Palmer Tomkinson, a board member and Cazenove partner, had suggested to David Acland that I should join the board. Henderson had taken over the fund in 1948, since when it had evolved into a diversified investment trust. In 2001, I succeeded David Acland as chairman, where I remained until 2012. Electric and General was a blue-chip investment trust, managed by Henderson, and for my first five years it was all plain sailing. In 2007, however, world markets were struck by the subprime crisis which originated in the US, mainly from the wildly risky practice of securitising mortgage lending. This worldwide crisis, which very nearly overwhelmed the world banking system and led to huge strains on the euro, caused ten years of austerity in the UK, certainly contributing in due course to the UK referendum decision to leave the EU. Henderson, our managers, completely failed to foresee the coming storm, although one of our non-executive directors forecast it clearly. Jonathan Ruffer, our star recruit at Dunbar, whom I had invited to join the board of E&G several years earlier, foresaw the crisis. I remember walking with him round the old port at Marseilles in 2006, and he described the world banking system as a disaster waiting to happen. It was this bearish stance that established Ruffer as one of the most successful new investment management groups in the City.He kept his clients out of trouble and, made a sufficiently large fortune so as to enable him later to purchase 12 magnificent paintings by Zurbaran and save the Bishop's Palace at Bishop Aukland.

Henderson, however, had their house view of where the markets were headed, and were not persuaded that any drastic change in policy was necessary; in due course our investment performance deteriorated badly, and the discount to net asset value on our shares widened substantially. Inevitably, before long we received an informal takeover approach from an outfit which inspired no confidence on our board. After the usual manoeuverings, we took the decision to replace Henderson as managers, and to launch a tender offer in cash for some of our stock, to cheer up the shareholders. The new manager we chose was Taube Hodson Stonex. Nils Taube was a legendary City investor, and had been a non-executive director of E&G before I became chairman; we greatly valued his contribution.

Unfortunately, he retired from E&G and, before long, was prevailed upon to resign from THS, when John Hodson and Cato Stonex took over. Lacking Nils' flair and experience, they were unprepared for the tremendous upheaval in the financial markets, following the 2007 sub-prime crisis. Performance suffered, and once again the discount widened ominously.

This led to a further take over approach from JP Morgan Overseas Trust, headed by George Paul, chairman of Aviva, whom I knew socially. Their own shares stood at nil discount, and they assured us that this situation would continue indefinitely. Once again, we were unpersuaded (we were correct; they soon went to a discount of about 8%) and we decided, instead of selling to them, to unitize, offering cash to all shareholders who wished to come out at asset value. Alternatively, they could take a tax-free conversion into a new OEIC (open ended investment company) called Electric and General. In my view, these two options were more attractive for shareholders. I was much criticised in the City and the financial press for presiding over the demise of another blue-chip investment trust. However, we negotiated an attractive agreement with THS with a very low management fee; our shareholders who opted for cash did well in being able to sell unlimited quantities of their holding at asset value, without dealing costs. Admittedly they had to pay capital gains tax on the cash offer, but they did not pay on the shares they chose to retain, and never again will they have to sell shares at a discount to net asset value. I am convinced it was a good deal and, as a substantial shareholder, I was in good position to evaluate it.

I then felt that the moment had come, after twelve years, when I should resign from the company, and was succeeded as chairman by Gerry Aherne. Before long, the board replaced THS as managers with Troy, a new and up-and-coming group under the chairmanship of Jan Pethick, a personal friend. Although E&G is now a much smaller trust, being worth about £100 million as opposed to £500 million in its heyday (resulting from all the cash redemptions), our shareholders, who were our first concern, have done well.

I have concluded my business career with two small companies, in which I made a substantial investment and became chairman. One was called ServicePower up in

Stockport, near Manchester. They had a scheduling software package acquired from ICL. We inherited a bad management team, and after twelve years of endless difficulties and management upheavals, which consumed a lot of time and considerable amounts of money, we appointed as CEO a lively American lady called Marnie Martin, and she managed to turn the company round to the point where the business was saleable. We eventually sold out for cash 15 years later, to a US private equity firm at a barely respectable price. In fact, by then, the company was doing well and we didn't get enough for it, but the shareholders had had enough; they wanted out.

The other company in which I invested and became chairman for ten years, was called Bango, which is in the rapidly growing and highly competitive field of mobile phone payments. Bango was founded by Ray Anderson, who had previously created a company called IXI in Cambridge, operating in the field of graphical user interface software for the UNIX operating system. This had been one of the better investments of Sharp Technology, and I had great confidence in Ray and his colleague, Anil Malhotra, who also came across from IXI to Bango. It has been a successful investment and they have built up a unique position in enabling payment for apps on mobile phones, particularly games, to be paid for, bundled up and incorporated with the customer's phone bill. This has involved years of negotiation with mobile phone companies all over the world, integrating Bango software to make it applicable. Although setting up the software and operating contracts with so many companies over the world has been a protracted exercise, this proves to be a real barrier to entry for competitors and the company has now achieved critical mass. Enormous volumes of transactions are processed through Bango; the company is now running at an annual run rate of half a billion transactions per annum. I persuaded the company to go for a public listing, which enabled the VCs to get out, and has helped the company to make acquisitions and raise money very cheaply and flexibly. Bango is an entirely suitable company for the AIM market.

So, Bango and ServicePower were my final directorships. I was paid my final salary cheque by ServicePower just before the sale of the company in June 2016, 55 years after I drew my first salary cheque from Schroders. I don't mind admitting that I'm proud that various people have found it worthwhile to pay me all this time.

One curious epilogue to my working career has been two overtures I received from the newspaper industry. The first was from Roger Harrison, a director of the Trinity Group of papers, which owned the *Liverpool Echo* and quite a large number of provincial papers. They were looking for a chairman and I had lunch with Philip Graff, the CEO, up in Chester, where the headquarters were situated. In fact I was not in a position to take up their offer immediately because I'd already undertaken to be High Sheriff of Shropshire for twelve months. The company couldn't wait and chose someone else.

More significantly, I was approached by Bob Gavron, the retiring chairman of the Guardian Media Group (GMG). Bob was a very able and charismatic entrepreneur who

A Shaky Start and a Lot of Luck

had made a major fortune in the St Ives Group, which he grew into being the U.K.'s largest and most profitable printer. He was a short, slightly built man with frizzy grey hair and soulful brown eyes and looked rather like Harpo Marx. He had great charisma and was a big supporter of the arts, notably the National Gallery and the Royal Opera House, to whom he gave large sums; he also gave a highly publicised £500,000 to the Labour Party. Bob suggested that I might consider succeeding him as chairman of the Guardian Media Group, mainly on the grounds that I was supposed to know something about technology and the Guardian had some important decisions to make.

GMG had an unusual structure. It was wholly owned by the Scott Trust, a non-profit-making trust, the result of an extraordinary act of generosity by the Scott family in Manchester in 1936, who donated the whole enterprise to the trust. This structure was designed to ensure the paper's independence, and prevent it being bought out by the usual egoists and megalomaniacs who control most of the world's newspapers. Back in 2005, when Bob showed me the figures, *The Guardian* was making a very small profit, *The Observer* lost £10 million a year and the rest of the provincial newspapers, mainly in Manchester, made a bit of money. The precarious finances, however, had been rescued by a spectacularly successful investment which they had made in *AutoTrader*, the leading mart for buying and selling cars, mainly online, later to be owned by Apax.

After some thought, I expressed interest and was interviewed by Hugo Young, the then chairman of the Scott Trust, and a leading columnist on *The Guardian*. I heard no more for a bit, while presumably, other candidates on the shortlist were being considered. After a while, I suddenly got cold feet about the whole thing. The salary was to be £50,000 a year, and one inducement was said to be the opportunity to meet the Cabinet and top politicians, and generally mingle with the great and the good. However, I didn't like the prospect of frequent journeys up and down to London to referee disputes about the large salaries that journalists earn. I am wary of journalists generally (although I have several close friends from the media), and my technical expertise was perhaps not quite as extensive as Bob Gavron had made out. I wrote to Bob withdrawing my candidature and after a short while, the company appointed Paul Mynors, a City figure much loved by Labour politicians.

My decision turned out to be a good one. Within two years, the newspaper industry suffered catastrophic losses, as all the small advertisements, situations vacant, and the other ads, which had been mainstream revenue earners for the newspaper industry, migrated to the Internet. Circulation and advertising on newspapers has been devastated and few groups are now in a more parlous condition than *The Guardian*. Once again, I was lucky not to have been there.

Chapter Twenty
Wildlife Holidays

About thirty years ago, David Attenborough began his series of wildlife films on television. I started watching them, and was completely entranced. I then had no idea of the extraordinary biodiversity of the tropics, and the beauty of the deserts and the Arctic, not to mention the temperate fauna and flora of Europe. I have always been a keen countryman and, like many people with an interest in shooting, became fascinated with wildlife and the conditions in which it could flourish. The Attenborough films in which he brought to life so vividly the incredible beauty and variety of our planet, made a big impression on me. Sarah shares this enthusiasm and we began to go on extended holidays in Africa and Asia, which we would normally combine with visits to nature reserves and other wild places.

Over the last thirty years, we have made visits, normally in February and March, to many countries in Africa: Egypt, Ethiopia, Kenya, Tanzania, Rwanda, Zaire, Malawi, Botswana, Namibia, Zimbabwe and South Africa. In Asia we have had similar trips to Nepal, India, Sri Lanka, Thailand, Bhutan, China and, more recently, Australia and New Zealand. In recent years, we have become increasingly enthusiastic about South America, where we've visited Argentina, Chile, Brazil, Peru, Ecuador, Costa Rica, Belize, Mexico, Cuba and, indeed, the United States, although I was more often there on business. Several of these places, particularly Tanzania, Botswana, India and Brazil we've visited many times and come to know fairly well.

Wildlife Holidays

We have had some memorable adventures on these trips. In Botswana one year, our safari guide was a large bearded man called Mike Penman, who at one time had been a bouncer in a Johannesburg nightclub. He was based in Selinda in Botswana, which was a designated hunting area, and he seemed to take extraordinary risks with both himself and his clients. I remember us being led into the bush on foot, where we had seen a pride of lions earlier in the day and our small party suddenly found ourselves only fifty yards from two lionesses, who became visible through the scrub, sitting with their backs to us. They were upwind of us but could have turned around and seen us or, more probably, we could have been set upon by members of the pride that we had not seen. I remember being extremely alarmed, but Mike put his finger to his lips and walked very slowly backwards, followed by us and in due course we regained the Land Rover.

On the same day, we went out at night in his Land Cruiser to a place where and Mike had earlier spotted six young lion cubs, aged about a year, nearly fully grown and already dangerous. It was pitch dark, and suddenly six pairs of eyes revealed that the cubs were just in front of us. Mike stopped the car, turned the engine off, got out and belly crawled along the track a few yards and lay face down, surrounded by the cubs bathed in our headlights. He lay completely motionless, and the cubs became increasingly curious, with Mike occasionally making tiny squeaks, causing them to draw ever closer, one touching his shoulder. The mother could have returned at any time, and would have killed him instantly. But she didn't, and

A Shaky Start and a Lot of Luck

for about fifteen minutes the rest of us, sitting ten yards behind in the Land Cruiser, enjoyed this extraordinary spectacle.

Another memorable visit was to Rwanda, where we went on holiday in search of the mountain gorillas. There are various groups of these animals, whose whereabouts are continuously known to the safari guides, and we were told that the usual favourites for the tourist groups were across the mountains in Zaire, as it then was. Then word came that a large group of 23 animals had been sighted near the border area, a considerable distance away. This involved spending the night on the mountain, Bisoke, in a primitive shack, but along with Simon and Amanda Cairns, our companions on the trip, we were up for it and we set off in the late afternoon on the long trek up to a hut set on a ridge deep in the rainforest, near the border with Zaire. After a completely sleepless night, during which we heard a profusion of forest sounds, at dawn there was a tap on our door and two safari guides appeared, and our adventure began. There followed an hour of incredibly tough walking behind our guides who were hacking away at the very thick undergrowth with their *pangas*, to open up a path. The vegetation was wet and thick, and we seemed to be constantly climbing in and out of ravines. From time to time we came across flattened areas of vegetation which, we were told, represented the resting place of the gorilla pack on previous nights. Finally, the front guide gave a little grunt and motioned to us to freeze. Sure enough, fifty yards ahead was a small gorilla playing around in the early morning light. Moving forward extremely slowly, before long the full pack came into view and for the next hour and a half we enjoyed the most incredible spectacle. Of all the Attenborough films, the footage of him being crawled over by baby gorillas is possibly the most famous. While we didn't get quite as close as that, we did get very near, assisted periodically by reassuring grunts from the guides. We were told to move extremely slowly and deliberately and not to use flash photography, and we came very close to 23 animals, with the male silverback weighing about 36 stone providing the central attraction. Sarah and I have some photographs of this and we will never forget the experience.

Then came the interminable descent of the mountain, down the wet and slippery gorges that led eventually to some potato fields, which bordered the reserve. Finally, about twelve hours later, we returned to the base camp more exhausted than I think I've ever been before or since.

There were many similar adventures on our holidays. Seeing the vast herds of wildebeest in the Serengeti National Park in Tanzania, was a great experience, which we have enjoyed about three times. In South Africa, we were invited to stay as guests by Roger and Annie Gabb, who took us whale watching. This involved a trip in a small boat to see whales and great white sharks. The whales are Southern Right Whales, whose cows swim up 1,000 miles from Antarctica to have their calves, just off the beaches of Hermanos near Cape Town. The adult female whale weighs about 50 tonnes, and our boat approached cautiously, stopping about 200 yards short of the mother, to assess her mood. We were lucky, and she slowly swam right up to our small rubber boat and, at one stage, we looked with some alarm at the spectacle of the huge tail emerging from the water on one side, and massive head and tiny inscrutable eyes on the other. Her body was right beneath our dinghy. The calf was by her side, and we remained for about 15 minutes, watching them at incredibly close range. If the mother whale had changed her mind about us, we could have been flipped into the freezing water in seconds. The Southern Right Whale is a considerable success story for the international whaling agreement. The population had got down to about 700 animals and today it is well over 7,000. They are certainly earning their keep as a tourist attraction. We also saw a number of great white sharks on the same trip. At one time, I counted four swimming round the boat; we were close to an island which contains a colony of about 50,000 seals, which are the main prey of the sharks.

One other travel incident, unconnected with wildlife, merits a mention. Sarah and I had joined a small group visiting a place called Xishuangbanna, in south west China, on the border with Laos and Thailand. There was some magnificent forest there, which inevitably was under threat, this time from rubber plantations. We stayed in very primitive forest lodges that were unbelievably dirty, with horrible food, accompanied by foresters clad in Chairman Mao boiler suits, who spent much of meal times spitting; the mess on the floor after dinner was most conveniently hoovered up by rats each night. Definitely not somewhere I would recommend for a honeymoon! One of our companions was called John MacKinnon, a colourful character, and passionate naturalist. One morning, after we'd eaten our revolting breakfast, it was time for the after-breakfast evacuations to take place. The lavatory was particularly impressive. It stood in the middle of quite a large room, like a throne, set in the concrete floor, with no cover on the cistern, which was erupting like a volcano. Accompanied by bubbles and gurgles, the water was rising like a mini fountain and the prospect of performing on this thing was daunting, to say the least. John, being the bravest of us, volunteered to be the first to go and he approached the lavatory and sat on it, getting soaked from the water descending on him from behind. In due course, 'le moment critique' arrived and John flushed. Immediately the ceiling gave way, and what must have been a substantial water tank disgorged its contents in a wall of water which completely engulfed John, to the point where he was invisible. It was an unforgettable moment; I don't think I've ever laughed so much.

Although wildlife and nature have provided the main attraction of most of our holidays, we have also enjoyed very much the conventional tourist attractions such as the Taj Mahal and the great palaces of India, and awe-inspiring spectacles, such as Machu Picchu and the Iguacu Falls of Brazil. In India, Sarah and I once went on holiday in Rajasthan with two additional ladies, Carolyn Sheffield and Susie Aird. We found ourselves as guests of two brothers, in a very run-down palace in a very poor area of the state. We were entertained the first evening by some dancers from the village, who moved beautifully and hypnotically, but were incredibly thin with huge dark eyes.

Malnutrition was rife in the area and apparently the diet consisted of nothing but chapattis and chillies. After an entertaining day around the palace and the grounds, during which our boat sank in a shallow lake, accompanied by much wringing of hands from the watching brothers, our girls were then invited to have a massage, accompanied by some opium to chew. This was followed by a fashion show with some beautiful saris, which they all bought. Sarah also bought a cat suit (for £2!) because we were giving a fancy dress party at Millichope the next month. The suit lasted one evening before falling apart; you get what you pay for!

We rose the following day, to be served breakfast on the roof of the palace. Two young Indians brought breakfast, one of whom was dressed in a magnificent white Rajput tunic, buttoned to the neck, with white jodhpurs, and a long flowing turban in vermilion, orange and brick red colours. It was my turn for a flash of inspiration: the fancy dress party at Millichope was imminent, and I still didn't have a costume for it. This would fit the bill perfectly. I asked the elder boy whether the younger one would be prepared to sell me his outfit; I was slimmer then and thought I could just about squeeze into it. My offer provoked a frantic whispered conversation between the two of them, and the reply came back in the affirmative. How much would they like to charge? This brought about further frenzied whisperings, following which, very sheepishly, a figure was mentioned. It was, of course, when translated into pounds, a derisory sum and I accepted immediately. Whereupon, both boys rolled their brown eyes in sheer happiness that anybody would pay their price without haggling. I don't know who was the keener, the buyer or the seller. In any case, I became possessed of a magnificent authentic Rajput outfit; my only problem was how to tie the turban, which was very long. They had shown me how to do it but, of course, when the time came, I'd forgotten. I wasn't too worried, however, because I was reasonably sure that somewhere in Birmingham I could find an Indian who could tie a Rajput turban; in fact it was done by a theatrical costumier from the Birmingham Rep. I think by general consent, I cut a dash at the party!

Despite other attractions, however, nature and wildlife above all have been the prime attraction on our travels, and this has led me over the years to becoming active in a number of conservation organisations, which keep me busy to this day.

Chapter Twenty-One
FFI, GCP, REGUA and TRINITY

I have spent a good deal of time and money on nature charities. At first, I was wary of many of these organisations, which appeared to be full of bunny huggers and muesli eaters, with unrealistic and sentimental notions about nature. After considerable deliberation, however, I decided to join the World Wildlife Fund (later to be known as the Worldwide Fund for Nature), and served there as a trustee for six years. The early years were interesting and rewarding, until WWF seemed to lose direction and after six years I resigned. The chairman, when I first joined, was Gerry Norman, who worked well with the director, George Medley; WWF UK grew substantially, becoming the most successful NGO in the international WWF family. Under Martin Laing, his successor, it lost its way and effective leadership; meetings were badly chaired, with too much time being given to time-wasters, and much of the agenda was often undiscussed at the end of meetings. More importantly, the structure of WWF, whereby each national NGO remitted most of the money they raised to a central organisation called IUCN, at Gland in Switzerland, was deeply flawed. Gland spent the money, which had been painstakingly raised, mainly in the UK and the Netherlands and this aroused resentment as well as an overlap in donations. Even worse was a schism that developed between Europe and the US; the US went its own way and were partners only in name, and the trustees in the US, unlike Europe, paid themselves handsome salaries.

FFI, GCP, REGUA and TRINITY

Bureaucracy, and an expensive, cumbersome overlap in functions further reduced effectiveness, and politics began to creep in. It was time to move on.

I resigned and joined Fauna and Flora International, where I was chairman for ten years, then president for another ten. FFI is the oldest wildlife conservation organisation in the world. Founded in 1903, it was originally called the Society for the Preservation of the Fauna and Flora of the British Empire. It was founded mainly by big-game hunters from the British aristocracy, although the American President, Teddy Roosevelt, was also a member. They were probably feeling some unease at the number of lions and elephants and other species that they were slaughtering; they were in fact lampooned in the British press as the Penitent Butchers. Whatever the reason, they had taken a belated interest in the preservation of big game in Africa.

During most of the last century, FFI was a very small-scale affair with a handful of staff, although with considerable influence worldwide. It was instrumental in setting up the Serengeti Park in Tanzania and, indeed, in the establishment of the World Wildlife Fund, with Peter Scott as its first chairman. I had been approached by Rudolph Agnew, a WWF board member, to see if I would be interested in becoming chairman of FFI. I expressed interest, and was interviewed in a tiny basement beneath the Royal Geographic Society in Kensington. The director at the time was Mark Rose, with a board of trustees mainly composed of academics in zoology and botany, and a staff of nine people. Now, 30 years later, Mark is still the director, having presided over an enormous growth in headcount, finances and major conservation achievements all over the world. FFI have had some remarkable successes; they rescued the Arabian oryx from extinction, by rounding up animals in the wild, where they were being persecuted by Arab hunters, and adding more from private collections, then relocating them in a desert in Arizona where conditions were comparable, before successfully reintroducing them to the Arabian Peninsula. The most spectacular achievement of all, however, has been with the mountain gorillas of Rwanda, Congo and Uganda. These magnificent creatures were in a desperate state, their numbers falling to about 400 and their habitat, subjected to continuous encroachment, reducing alarmingly. They live in rainforest on a spectacular mountain range, surrounded by some of the most densely populated areas of the world. Poaching and trapping had decimated the population, and cultivation of the highly-fertile land adjoining the forest was continuously moving uphill into the reserved area. It is wonderful to record that, despite a vicious civil war in the immediate vicinity between the Hutu and the Tutsi tribes, which ultimately cost a million lives, the gorilla population has now grown to 900 animals and, with the establishment of a reserve, currently a significant foreign currency earner for Rwanda, but also extending into Zaire and Uganda. The gorillas' prospects for the time being now look much better. Dianne Fossey can sleep more easily in her grave.

Mark is the most successful and respected director in the conservation movement in the UK. I worked very closely

FFI, GCP, REGUA and TRINITY

with him in all the years I was chairman, and then president, and he remains a good friend to this day. Through most of the nineties, FFI was living on a shoestring. We were always trying to do more than we could afford, but there was so much to be done! At one stage, our unrestricted reserves almost disappeared and we were worried that the Charity Commission might come after us. However, among other donors, a fairy godmother arrived in the shape of Lisbet Rausing, daughter of Hans Rausing, the Swedish founder of Tetra Pak, whose best-known product was the milk pack container. Lisbet approached us and decided we were the conservation organisation with whom she wished to work. The result was the Arcadia Fund, which started at $5,000,000 and has since grown to $25,000,000. The Arcadia Fund seeks to acquire pristine, but endangered habitats all over the world, to protect and manage them. This is managed on the ground by FFI, and it has now become a major enterprise. Lisbet's example has been followed by many other donors, and FFI has become a worldwide organisation with a turnover of £20 million and 180 employees.

I worked continuously to try and raise money for FFI, and supported Mark's efforts to work with major industrial corporations, both in raising funds, and influencing their operations in environmentally sensitive areas. We could have been criticised for working with companies such as British Petroleum and British American Tobacco, but we took the view that partnering was much better than criticism. We were never a charity raising funds from the general public, and we could take a bit of flak.

A Shaky Start and a Lot of Luck

Finally, the time came for me to move on and hand over the chair. Rather immodestly, I would like to quote from a letter written to me on my giving up the chair of FFI while I was president. It was from Sir David Attenborough.

Dear Lindsay

I would like to take this opportunity to thank you for your support to the charity in 2007 2008 and 2009, through your most generous membership of the conservation circle and of course your service as our President. With your support, the Conservation Circle has now contributed over three quarters of £1 million to underpin FFI's work, thus helping to save species from extinction and habitats from destruction whilst improving the livelihoods of many poor communities. This is a tremendous achievement and I offer you a heartfelt thanks.

It is so important that those of us who value the natural world for its own sake continue to take action to ensure that its conservation is kept high on the agenda. I have been involved with FFI for over 50 years and I believe strongly that it has a unique role to play in addressing global conservation issues, and that FFI gets results.

Although the threats are great, if we care about our planet, then we have to do something to protect it. It is wonderful that you been able to pledge support from the Millichope Foundation for conservation circle membership up to 2012. As FFI stands poised to rise to the challenges

FFI, GCP, REGUA and TRINITY

facing the planet, your support of its marvellous work has never been more essential.

With my sincere thanks
David Attenborough.

To have received such a letter from the man who I possibly admire more than anybody in the world was quite overwhelming. It remains a treasured possession.

After my time at FFI came to an end, I was still keen to be involved in conservation and became chairman of the Global Canopy Programme (GCP) and Brazilian Atlantic Rainforest Trust (BART).

Global Canopy was founded in 1995 by Andrew Mitchell. As the name suggests, the initial objective was to build walkways through the canopy of the rainforest. It has changed direction several times, and now is primarily a lobbying organisation that seeks to influence governments as well as large retailers and manufacturers in Europe, the USA and elsewhere, to try and preserve the world's rainforests by promoting best practice in buying forest products from sustainable sources.

Global Canopy has recently adopted a product called TRASE. This uses some sophisticated Swedish-developed software, which enables us to illustrate to major consuming companies that use palm oil, soy or other commodities, whether these have come from a sustainable and responsibly produced source. We provide the tools which help them to establish the facts. It is particularly encouraging that many of the world's major investing institutions now take a real interest in these matters, and

A Shaky Start and a Lot of Luck

Natural Capital is moving rapidly up on the list of priorities of most major multinationals. We help them to find out where their products are coming from, and to place themselves in a position to respond to criticism from their shareholders, as well as making changes where necessary. GCP has also done some valuable pioneering work on establishing carbon offsets, as a means of limiting the growth of CO_2 in the atmosphere.

Finally, the Brazilian Atlantic Rainforest Trust has been a huge success and I have found it particularly rewarding. It was started by the Locke family, who were Anglo-Brazilian farmers, living on their farm about two hours' drive north east of Rio de Janeiro. It is the most spectacularly beautiful place, and about 20 years ago, Nicholas Locke and his father, Robert met Sir Ghillean (Ian) Prance, who was at that time, the director of Kew Gardens in London. Together with two passionate birdwatchers, Stephen Rumsey and Tasso Leventis, and two or three others, they all decided to form a nature reserve on the farm. Both Nicholas, his wife Raquel, and his father Robert were keen to establish a reserve, which was called REGUA (Reserva Ecologica de Guapiaçu). Guapiaçu refers to the river flowing through the centre of the reserve and into Guanabara Bay, just by Rio airport. The objective was to plant native forest trees; the reserve is situated in one of the last remaining areas of the Brazilian Atlantic Rainforest, quite distinct from the Amazon Rainforest, and even richer in biodiversity and more acutely threatened. A small lodge was built to accommodate parties of birdwatchers, mainly from Europe, but now increasingly from Brazil. A significant area of existing rainforest was included in the reserve stretching up a steep escarpment towards the 6,000-foot peaks of the mountain range.

I came to know Ian Prance on a holiday on the Amazon, and he invited me to become a trustee of BART in 2006. After about five years, he decided to resign and the trustees invited me to succeed him as chairman. Every two years, Sarah and I go out to Brazil, which we love, and have derived deep satisfaction from watching the reserve expand and carry out its planting programmes, establishing wetlands and undertaking education and training for the surrounding schools. We have now planted nearly 500,000 trees from among 200 different species growing in the hills above the reserve. This target of half a million will be reached this year.

At the same time, we've bought a lot more land, assisted by the weakness of the Brazilian real, and we now own or manage 11,400 hectares. A significant proportion of our costs is now covered by receipts from bird watching tourists, and it is very satisfying that Nicholas and Raquel's son and daughter, Tom and Michaela, are now both working in the reserve. We have even had parties of insect lovers; there is a bug wall in the garden, which is a large white surface with a powerful light shining on it. Very large numbers of an incredible variety of insects cling to the wall dazzled by the light. One of the guests filled up a jar full of bugs which he took up to his bedroom for the night (I don't think his wife was too pleased!). He had, of course, to release them back into the wild the following morning. Poachers from the villages up and down the valley used to be active, but now several of them are employed by us as rangers and bird watching guides. Our efforts have come to the attention of the authorities in Rio de Janeiro, who are belatedly becoming alarmed about the security of their water supply, and the generally polluted state of Guanabara Bay into which the Guapiaçu flows. I hope that before long we will receive some tangible encouragement from the Brazilian authorities, since we are already attracting widespread attention as a best-of-breed conservation organisation. Two things I particularly like about REGUA as a charity is first, that every penny of money we raise goes straight to the reserve without intermediaries or any layers of administration, and secondly, Nicholas and Raquel, with assistance from the admirable Alan Martin, our company secretary and director, run the reserve with real passion and dedication, and account to the trustees closely for everything that goes on.

It is just as well that there are one or two success stories in conservation because, globally, the picture is thoroughly depressing. All the major mammals in the wild are in varying degrees of trouble, and the same goes for large numbers of birds, reptiles and marine life. Overpopulation and the understandable desire for higher standards of living, has set human beings on a collision course with the sustainability of the planet. Whether it be massive farming organisations in Brazil destroying the Amazon forest for timber, cattle and soya, or subsistence farming in the tropics, wherever nature stands in the way of somebody making money, or, indeed, scratching a living, nature loses every time. The pace of destruction in my lifetime has been devastating. In the last seventy years, tigers, lions, elephants, cheetahs and rhinoceros, to name but a handful of flagship species, are now critically endangered. Since the Second World War, and the worldwide boom in population and increased living standards, it has all happened incredibly rapidly. Even insects are now under pressure from the huge spread of pesticides, and the oceans are being devastated by pollution and overfishing.

About five years ago, we visited Ethiopia where, since the Second World War, the forested area of the country has shrunk from one third to one twentieth, while the population has doubled to about 100 million. Subsistence farming has replaced the forests, and the only trees to be seen in most villages are mutilated eucalyptus. Before long, Ethiopia, particularly in the northern areas, together with Eritrea, Somalia and Sudan, will be unable to sustain current populations and significant numbers are already desperately trying to get into Europe. It is a catastrophic situation that was entirely predictable, but I have been astonished by how soon it has happened.

These are sombre topics, but would be a mistake to think that all is doom and gloom; attitudes are changing, particularly among young people. In fact, for some of them, ecological issues seem to have supplanted religion, as is shown by the large numbers of ideologically motivated young people, who work for very little money in these voluntary organisations in which I have served. I have been encouraged and inspired in getting to know them.

During the summer of 1995, Grey Gowrie, who had been Mrs Thatcher's Minister for the Arts, came to dinner at Millichope. I was toying with the idea of becoming a trustee of an orchestra, but then it occurred to me that involvement with a major teaching organisation or academy would be more interesting. I discussed this with Grey and, before long, I received a telephone call from Gavin Henderson, the principal of Trinity College of Music in London. I went to see him at his office in Marylebone, and was pleased to find a highly entertaining and charismatic man, with a fund of good stories and penchant for large, flamboyant bow ties. Gavin's instrument turned out to be the French horn and he was lamenting the fact that his set of horns had just been stolen. We went off to the Savile Club and, at the end of a very good lunch during which Gavin was at his most persuasive, I agreed to become a member of the development committee.

Trinity had a problem. Their leases in Marylebone were coming to an end, and they had to move. By far the most attractive option, and one that the trustees were on the verge of adopting, was to move to the King Charles Court of the Royal Palace at Greenwich. This was an exciting project and, although moving out of central London is not without risk, half the palace was already part of Greenwich University and King Charles Court – the west wing – could be converted into a magnificent music academy. The problem was that the move would cost £15 million: £9 million would come from the sale of the unexpired leases in Marylebone and a further £4 million from the Higher Education Funding Council of England (HEFCE). This left £2 million and this was where I came in. I scratched my head a bit because this was a large sum. But then

FFI, GCP, REGUA and TRINITY

I remembered meeting a man called Alan Grieve on a shoot in Shropshire. Alan was the chairman of the Jerwood Foundation. This was a foundation that was established in 1977 for John Jerwood to support, first of all, education and then, increasingly, the arts. Jerwood had made a sizeable fortune in cultured pearls in the Far East and had left no heir. Following his death the direction and management went to Alan, who was a family friend and lawyer. The funds are managed and controlled offshore and they had made substantial donations to the arts over a number of years (£100 million since 1991), one of them being the Jerwood Theatre at the Royal Court in Sloane Square. With some difficulty, I managed to set up an appointment with Alan and, when the day came, Gavin and I went to the Jerwood HQ in Fitzroy Square. We were shown into an attractive room full of mid-20th century English paintings and had about fifteen minutes to admire them before the great man arrived. After the introductions and preliminaries, Gavin explained that we were looking for a contribution to close the £2 million gap. It became clear, however, that Alan was not in the least interested in participating in a general funding. That was not Jerwood's style. What they wanted was a bespoke Jerwood branded project. Gavin saw the way the wind was blowing and adroitly changed tack.

Trinity had been offered a unique collection of playbills and show posters and theatrical memorabilia from the beginning of the 20th century, known as the Mander and Mitchenson Collection. What about acquiring the collection and housing it in a special section of the college, and

A Shaky Start and a Lot of Luck

calling it the Jerwood Library at Trinity? He suggested. Alan liked this much better and, after many months of negotiation and refining the project, he offered £1 million. It was this donation which made the decisive difference that enabled Trinity to move.

The actual move was memorable. On a beautiful sunny, autumn day, two large barges made a procession from Charing Cross Pier to Greenwich. The Festival Hall illuminated their panel overlooking the Thames with 'Good Luck Trinity.' Later, a mile or so downstream, Tower Bridge raised the bridge to allow us through. We then arrived at Greenwich to be met by hundreds of mainly black schoolchildren, waving flags and welcoming placards. Finally, we assembled for a great reception at the Painted Hall in the Palace. It was quite a day.

My fundraising efforts were not quite complete. Trinity were unable to move their organ from Marylebone to Greenwich and a new one had to be commissioned. It was to be a beautiful chamber organ made by William Drake, to be situated in the Peacock Room in King Charles's Court. The bill was £135,000. I suddenly remembered that the most famous organ teacher at Trinity had been Harry Gabb. He was much loved and well-remembered for his outstanding contribution to the college. He was also organist at St Paul's Cathedral. It just so happened that his adopted son, Roger Gabb, is a very close friend of mine, a neighbour in Shropshire, and had recently made a very large sum of money by selling his wine business. I wrote to Roger explaining the situation and the daunting sum that had to be raised. Roger wrote back almost by return of post offering to cover the lot. It was his own money and a magnificent gesture. The inaugural recital took place with Katherine Ennis on our beautiful new organ, and it was a great occasion.

It was ironic that two of the most significant gifts to the college came from Shropshire! Shropshire funding London doesn't seem quite right, but that's how it worked out.

Chapter Twenty-Two
The Millichope Foundation

So far this story has been mainly about my career in business and making money. On the whole, this has been successful, and from the early 80s, I did find that I had funds over and above my own pressing needs and, indeed, those of the Millichope and Ruantallain Estates. I hadn't previously thought a great deal about charity, and had simply responded to various appeals and other solicitations that came my way. In 1982, however, Sarah and I decided to set up our own small charity, which we called a little pompously the Millichope Foundation.

Increasingly, when wandering around the streets of some big city and encountering people with dreadful deformities being wheeled about by relatives or carers, it struck me what amazing good fortune I had had in life, and how thankful I was that I was not similarly indisposed or, indeed, in a position of having to devote most hours in the day to looking after disabled dependants. I have never been particularly tempted by yachts, racehorses, gambling or most of the usual ways of getting through money and as the saying goes, 'You can only eat three meals a day.'

We came to the realisation that we had enough to be able to afford to give some away. So the Millichope Foundation was started in 1982, on a very small scale. The opening capital was £10,000, and we gave away quite modest sums. Before long, however, the Foundation grew rapidly, and this was to a considerable extent made possible by the UK tax system. Capital Gains Tax (CGT) for

The Millichope Foundation

much of the eighties and nineties, when I was realising some large gains, was 40%. I had the strongest objection to paying such high rates and I preferred to give away shares on which I already had a substantial unrealised capital gain, to the Foundation. This manoeuvre meant there was no tax payable, because gifts to charity were exempt from CGT.

In recent years, this route has become even more attractive because, although CGT, thankfully, has come down, gifts attract gift aid, which is now deducted from my income tax bill. Since the 80s and 90s were good years for the stock market, I transferred substantial sums to the Foundation. Indeed, the assets of the charity now exceed £8,500,000, and we have additionally paid out over £6,000,000 in donations.

Another attraction for me has been being able to control investment policy, and I think the Foundation's investments have performed well, probably better than could have been achieved by a conventional investment manager. We started out purely investing in stocks and shares. But in recent years the portfolio has diversified and we have acquired a farm and a portfolio of flats in the middle of Birmingham. Our income has grown to about £330,000 a year. For many years Sarah and I were the only trustees, but we were joined in due course by Bridget Marshall, our family solicitor, and recently, our children, Frank and Harriet. Although it may sound a bit incestuous, with all the money having come from the Bury family, none of the trustees are paid, and we only give money away to other registered charities. The main beneficiaries have been

A Shaky Start and a Lot of Luck

Shropshire charities, which account for about half. Shropshire is a large county, but with a small population, and it is not well served by public services. It has some wonderful old buildings that need maintenance, together with some of the most beautiful landscapes in Britain, to which we have contributed towards helping to keep them unspoiled, so far as possible. Then there are the usual social causes, with respite care and charities for the disabled, featuring prominently. I think the Foundation in a small way meets an important need in the county, particularly with local authority finance in such a parlous state. Although many friends and neighbours are well-off in terms of land, there is not much free cash about for charities. We have also given quite large sums to environmental charities, particularly where, in some cases, I have served as trustee and chairman, and finally, a certain amount towards the arts. We also have, of course, our pet favourites, which we have supported for many years.

Typically, we give five-year donations of quite modest sums to a large number of small charities, generally in Shropshire. This enables them to plan ahead, and regular donations are in some cases preferable to large one-off sums. There is no legal obligation to continue the payments if, for some reason, we want to discontinue them. We have had a wonderful secretary and clerk in Sue Kerr, and two ladies, Ann Crutwell and Frances Barlow, who have played a useful role in visiting specific charities that we think sound promising, but which require further investigation. Running the Foundation has been rewarding and satisfying, although the sheer number of envelopes that arrive every day from charities all over the country does require a certain amount of work in sifting and evaluation. I like to think that we have made a difference to some beneficiaries. Now that Frank and Harriet are trustees, I very much hope that under their guidance, together with the other trustees, the Millichope Foundation will be a lasting asset to Shropshire, and to other charities in years to come.

Over the years I have also become personally involved in the voluntary sector. I was for twelve years chairman of the governors of Moor Park, a Catholic preparatory school near Ludlow, where both of our two children and all of our seven grandchildren have been pupils. Derek Henderson and subsequently, John Badham were the two headmasters during my time as chairman. Derek was one of the founders of the school and a charismatic character. He and his partner, Hugh Watts, established the school as a Catholic boys' boarding prep school. They had friends who sent their sons to the school and since they were both good cricketers and sportsmen, Moor Park in its early years, excelled at games, considering its small size. As Hugh and Derek grew older, so did their friends, and the number of parents likely to send their sons to the school diminished, while the costs of boarding prep schools remorselessly increased; it became clear that the school needed a change of direction, which meant first of all, taking girls and secondly, day children.

All of this pointed to the need for a new headmaster and, by then, first Hugh, then Derek, wished to retire. I had to negotiate severance arrangements with them, and then preside over the choice of a new headmaster. The various candidates were mostly unimpressive, probably due to the stipulation that we only wanted a Catholic, which obviously narrowed the field. We chose John Badham, who interviewed well, coming from a school in North London which was a co-educational, day school with no fixed religious affiliation, although, in fact, John was a devout Catholic. It was not an easy selection, and the governors were split over it. I was strongly in favour of John, who was by head and shoulders the strongest candidate, and fortunately we prevailed. For many years he did us very well indeed. The numbers built up and, before long, there were as many girl pupils as boys. Moor Park remained a Catholic school in spirit and the wonderful happy atmosphere which prevailed under Derek, survived very well under John. Pastoral care was one of our strengths. The trouble, however, with day children is that they bring in less money than boarders, and throughout my tenure as chairman, the annual surplus grew less and less, and for all capital items, we had to rely on appeals and donations.

After a long spell of 12 years, at the end of which John Badham moved on, I gave up the chair. It was time for a new board of governors who would relate more closely to the younger generation of parents. Above all I did not think it was appropriate that I should be choosing the new headmaster, knowing full well that I planned to retire very soon, and would not have to live with the consequences of my decision. I'm delighted to say that, several years later, Moor Park is doing very well. I go to football and cricket matches to watch my grandsons and granddaughters in action, and have much enjoyed cold, wet winter afternoons, yelling support at almost indistinguishable muddy children. I have also made friends with many of the new parents who are also close friends of Frank and Harriet's, one of whom, Susie Allan, now gives me piano lessons.

I have also spent some time on Ludlow charities, notably the Fabric Trust of St Laurence's Church, a truly wonderful church whose tower dominates the town. I believe we have repaired the pinnacles and made a start on the roof during my time as trustee. One of our appeals involved a 24-hour continuous, round-the-clock recital of songs, poetry or some other performance. My slot on the rota was 4am, and I massacred various golden oldies at the piano in front of an heroic audience of twelve. At least at that time of night I could find somewhere to park!

More recently, I have been for six years a trustee of the Ludlow Assembly Rooms. The time I was there was dominated by an ambitious scheme to refurbish the handsome 18th century building, on the south side of Castle Square. The plan was to convert the ground floor, changing the entrance from Mill Street to the square, and introducing a restaurant on the corner. This has involved extensive and tortuous negotiations with our landlord, Shropshire County Council, and at last the first stage of a deal has now happily been signed, which has unlocked a significant grant from Europe. However, considerable work and effort is still needed to complete the whole thing.

Chapter Twenty-Three
The Family

Our two children, Frank and Harriet were brought up at Millichope. They influenced the way we lived in that large house; the nursery, which had been designed by the architect, was upstairs in the opposite corner of the house and was soon abandoned for the kitchen and, indeed, the grand rooms. Frank, aged six, became pretty adept at skateboarding round the hall, something which attracted criticism from one pompous grandee of the Georgian Society. They were very much country children, starting at the village school in Munslow, where they made many local friends, before going on to Moor Park, followed by Eton for Frank and St Mary's, Calne for Harriet.

Harriet – she would be the first to admit – was a nightmarish teenager, and managed to persuade us that she should leave St Mary's and come home to go to the sixth form at Shrewsbury High School, where she acquired some unsavoury boyfriends. She wore dreadlocks and Doc Marten boots, and used to call me a money-grubbing capitalist which, in retrospect, seems fair enough, although I didn't appreciate hearing it at the time.

She spent her gap year in India and it was there, in 1990, that she had an appalling car accident. She was in a taxi near Manali in the Kulu Valley in the Himalayas. The cause of the accident was not entirely clear, but the car in which she was a passenger, probably had defective brakes and maybe the driver was not paying attention. Whatever the reason, the taxi rolled down a ravine turning over five times

The Family

before a door flew open, which arrested the fall on the edge of a further drop into a river. She was thrown clear, unconscious and critically hurt. She was then picked up, carried up to the road and dumped into another taxi, eventually to be taken to the Lady Willingdon Hospital in Manali. We received a telephone call from her travelling companion over a week later, giving us, over a crackling telephone line, the skimpiest details of what had happened.

We were appalled and immediately contacted the travel insurance company, who told us that, rather than travelling out to India, the best thing we could do was to stay at home by a telephone. This we did, and we had to follow events from a distance for nearly three weeks. The first ten days she lay immobile in Manali, where she was under the care of the remarkable Dr Larghi Varghese, a Christian doctor from Southern India. He was in charge of the Lady Willingdon Hospital and has since featured prominently in our lives. From Manali she was taken down to Delhi to the East West Medical Centre, where she had to spend a week, because it coincided with Rajiv Gandhi's assassination and subsequent curfew, and no seats were available on flights to London. Finally, she did get on a flight to Gatwick; British Airways had to allocate nine seats to accommodate her stretcher, and an accompanying Indian doctor. I shall never forget seeing her in the back of an ambulance at Gatwick, overjoyed to have her back but shocked at how thin she had become. Sarah travelled in the ambulance with her to the Orthopaedic Hospital in Oswestry, Shropshire, where she was placed under the care of Dr Wagih El Masri. She was then further immobilized, with calipers attached to her head for six weeks, while she was able to move only her eyeballs. How she didn't go mad, I'll never know but, after the six weeks, they were removed and she was eventually able to stand, having had gradually to relearn how to walk. She did, in due course, make an almost full recovery, though she had lost 20% of the capacity of her spinal cord. It was, in my view, a miracle.

After her period of recuperation, Harriet went to SOAS (the School of Oriental and African studies, part of London University, where she took a First Class degree). She then went to Queen Mary's, where she got a Masters in 18thcentury European philosophical history. After a year as an editorial assistant at Thames and Hudson, the publishers in Bloomsbury, she resumed her academic path, with funding for a PhD at SOAS in 19th-century Indian history. She's a bright girl.

While at Thames and Hudson, she had an interesting conversation with one of her colleagues from the Victorian Society who asked her where she lived.

'In Shropshire,' she replied.

'Oh, how nice; where in Shropshire?'

'Near Ludlow.'

'Oh, that's the nicest part of Shropshire. Where, near Ludlow?'

'Just near a village called Munslow, in the Corvedale,' Harriet said.

'What a coincidence! We went there the other day and there is a beautiful house, called Millichope and some buffoon has completely ruined it by burying Haycock's Doric columns between mounds of earth works.'

The Family

'That was my dad!' Harriet admitted, sheepishly.

It just shows you can't please everybody!

She went on before long to get married to a charming, easy-going young man called Marshall Horne from London and, in due course, they had three children, Albert, Nell and Joy.

Harriet had caused us no small measure of anxiety and worry, but she's turned into a remarkable woman and wonderful mother. From her early hippy days in India, she has become a pillar of Shropshire society, living first up the hill behind our new home at the Old Rectory in Tugford, and now at The Manor House, Corfton, a beautiful 18th century house, with a lovely view of the Clee Hill. Her accident led to her playing a leading role in raising money for hospitals, not only the Lady Willingdon in Manali, but the Spinal Injuries Unit of the Orthopaedic Hospital in Oswestry. We love her living next door with her three wonderful children, Albert, who has just gone to Shrewsbury, and Nell and Joy, who are still at Moor Park.

For his part, Frank did very well at Eton, and got into the 1st XI at cricket (the first Bury to have achieved that since his great-grandfather). He then went to Manchester University, where he read history and got a good degree, to emerge on the job market in 1992. The early 90s was a period of recession and a tough time for a young graduate to get a job, and being an old Etonian didn't help at all. Reaction against elitist toffs had already started!

After being turned down at 22 interviews, by which time most his friends who were also job hunting, had got fed up and thrown in the sponge, Christopher Palmer-Tomkinson gave him an opening at Cazenove, the large blue-chip stockbroker in the City. So his first job started and before long he was sent to the Far East, where he soon found his feet, and began to do some useful work for the firm; he certainly pointed me in the direction of some useful stock market tips! He spent ten years at Cazenove, before moving to Sloane Robinson, a hedge fund where he worked for four years, before going to a business school, IESE, in Barcelona. There he got a broader trading and returned to establish his own venture capital company, BFLAP, an acronym for Bury, Fitzwilliam Lay Partners. Hugh Fitzwilliam Lay is Frank's brother-in-law, who had returned from a highly successful venture in New York, where he'd sold his courier business to the Royal Mail. The two of them went into partnership together.

Frank married Antonia Fitzwilliam Lay on 23 January 1999. This was a very happy day for Sarah and me. The Fitzwilliam Lay family live at Bloxham, near Great Bedwyn in the Savernake Forest in Wiltshire. David and Ann, Tonie's parents had five children and she was the youngest. She is a beautiful girl with a happy uncomplicated approach to life and she's been a wonderful addition to our family. She is also highly practical, whether with cars, computers or doing up houses, which is a perfect foil to the clumsiness and absent-mindedness of the Bury family. They started married life in a ground floor flat in Warwick Square, Pimlico, where their first child, Willa was born. When she was still a baby, they decided to embark on the adventure of moving to Barcelona, for Frank's MBA at IESE. Sarah's best friend from university in Dublin, Annette, is Frank's

The Family

godmother and she had married a Spaniard, a distinguished and charming academic, Juan Garcia de la Banda. Frank had spent his gap year in Madrid and has since developed a Spanish alter ego. He is fluent in Spanish (rather than Catalan) and Willa, to Frank's delight, is now studying Spanish A-level and has paid a couple of visits on her own to Annette's family. Lucas, our grandson, was born in Barcelona, and the family then returned to the UK and moved to the Old Rectory in Munslow, where Florence and Dora were born. All the grandchildren have started at the village school and from there progressed to Moor Park.

In the meantime, over a number of years, I transferred the whole of Millichope Estate to Frank, as well as the main house, Millichope Park, to where the family moved in 2009 and undertook a further substantial renovation of the house. They did this while occupying a wing, and it must have been a nightmare living in the middle of a building site for two years. However, they survived, and the work they had done has been very successful.

This refurbishment basically completed the unfinished renovation of the back of the house, which Sarah and I lacked the money and the energy to complete. Most notably, they have restored the original magnificent dining room, which we had reduced in size and divided in two. The work was extensive, almost comparable with the original project which Sarah and I had put in hand 40 years earlier, and it did take two years to complete. Sarah and I are really pleased with the changes to the house and I am hugely relieved that its future, and that of the estate, now look secure, politics permitting, for a few more years.

A Shaky Start and a Lot of Luck

Frank, ably assisted by Tonie, is running the estate very well and, being an Ingall, he has a good grasp of detail and thinks problems through thoroughly. I have always relied on land agents for the day-to-day running of the estate and, basically, it ticked over for the 40 years or so of my active business career. Frank has taken a much more hands-on approach.

One good example of the benefits of the change in management came fairly soon after he took over. We had a little business selling logs up and down the Corvedale from hardwood thinnings on the estate, and our customers nearly all paid cash. I should have realised that it is always a mistake to completely trust employees to handle cash. I was giving our head woodman a 5% cash bonus on receipts from the new venture but, before long he decided that 100% was much more interesting than 5%, and he started helping himself to about £5,000 a year. This went on for two or three years before Frank spotted it and undertook an exhaustive investigation, suffering many sleepless nights before he had sufficient information to confront the culprit. After a couple of meetings with the usual bluster and evasions, we had enough evidence to sack him. As soon as he went, sales of logs rose by 25% and morale all over the estate improved. One rotten apple is enough to contaminate a whole barrel, and Frank did a great job in rooting it out.

Since then, many good things have happened at Millichope, notably a renovation of the old curvilinear greenhouses in the walled garden, and the restoration of the line of cascades running down from the lower lake to the main road. This was very much a personal triumph of my wife, Sarah's, who supervised the whole scheme and negotiated a large grant from Natural England as part of our stewardship scheme for historic parkland. We have also created a wetland of about 12 acres, which has been adopted by a good population of breeding lapwing, as well as ducks, geese and snipe. This was designed by our keeper, Liam Bell, who, as well as being an outstanding gamekeeper, naturalist and countryman, is now an author and head of the National Gamekeepers Association.

More recently, he and Frank have embarked on an extensive project to reintroduce wild grey partridges to the estate, from where they had completely disappeared. I remember hearing the coveys chirping in the years after the war, and it gives me huge pleasure to think that native English partridges are now once again flourishing on Millichope estate. We have also extended a small area of wildflower meadows on the top of the Wenlock Edge, where they are returning in abundance. When the project is completed, we will have over 60 acres of pristine wildflower meadows, which is a worthwhile block. All this green activity is very trendy now and indications are that, following BREXIT, more money will be forthcoming for environmental work. It is satisfying, indeed, to be rewarded for work you enjoy doing, and have been doing for years.

Sarah and I have had a ringside seat on all this activity and we have really enjoyed having both families, the Burys and the Hornes, living within two or three miles, and seeing our grandchildren grow up. This surely is one of the best possible rewards for grandparents. We feel personally involved in the lives of all our seven grandchildren, whom we love greatly.

Chapter Twenty-Four
Music and Friends

Besides business, the environment and, of course, my family, music has always been a major interest for me. My father was a musician and I certainly inherited his love of music. As a young pianist, I was very poorly taught at school and equally badly at university, where I continued piano lessons. Later, when I was working, I didn't really have time to play much, and it is only in retirement that I have begun to have some decent lessons and learn how to practise properly. I have reached a standard where I can play with other musicians and, just occasionally, before an audience. There is, however, a long way to go!

I often wonder what would have happened if my father had not been killed when I was so young. Most likely, I would have followed in his footsteps, as many sons do, and gone into the music business. I would certainly never have made it as a performer. During my time on the development committee of the Trinity College of Music in London, I became aware of the influx of Far Eastern music students (upon which the finances of the colleges largely depend) and the incredible competition faced by any aspiring performer. It would be easier if the Asiatic students stuck to their own music but, unfortunately for our home-grown young talent, they seem to prefer Mozart and Beethoven! To succeed as a soloist nowadays is incredibly tough.

When living in London in the sixties, I went to hundreds of concerts, operas and ballets, and have strong memories of some great occasions: McCracken, the Canadian tenor flinging himself across the stage as a madly jealous *Otello*; Fonteyn and Nureyev performing for the first time in *Marguerite et Armand*, whirling around passionately above the tremendous chords of Liszt's Sonata in B minor; Callas singing *Norma* in the open-air Greek theatre at Epidaurus. What an electrifying figure she was, singing Casta Diva above the fading sound of the cicadas in the hills around the theatre, as darkness fell. Then there was a piano recital at the Festival Hall by Michelangeli, the Italian maestro, of two early Beethoven sonatas with Debussy's Préludes after the interval. The recital needed two pianos, one for Beethoven, the other for Debussy. After each prelude, the maestro would carefully mop his brow with a black silk handkerchief. At the conclusion of the recital, after one slow bow, he just stared at the audience with an expression of dislike and contempt, declining to play an encore. The tickets were massively expensive (£25 each! back in the sixties) but the slow movement of the Beethoven was unbelievable and the pianissimo playing of the Préludes I can still remember. The evening was worth every penny.

After moving back to Millichope, Sarah and I took to staging one, or sometimes two, concerts a year in our music room. The room had a good acoustic when full with an audience, and could seat 120 at full capacity. I found that I could charge quite modest ticket prices to local music lovers and yet afford some good players. We had many memorable evenings: Tony and Caroline Goldstone played most of the two-piano repertoire (at that stage we had two large pianos – besides my Steinway D model, I had a Weber, made in New York). Ian Partridge came with his sister Jenny and I shall never forget him singing *Youth and Love* from Vaughan Williams' *Songs of Travel*, the Joachim piano trio with Rebecca Hirsch, Caroline Deansley and John Lenahan performed most of the highlights of the piano Trio repertoire. It gives me great pleasure that Frank, since moving into Millichope, has continued the tradition of the concerts. He has made his own circle of musical friends and a new younger generation of performers have arrived on the scene, and very good they are too. My own piano teacher, Susie Allan, gave a concert accompanying Roderick Williams in Schubert's *Die Schöne Müllerin*. In addition to the top names, we also occasionally find time to stage smaller concerts for local amateur performers. I even once gave a concert myself, in conjunction with two excellent string players from the Ulster Orchestra. We played two Haydn piano trios finishing with the 'Gypsy' trio. The reader doesn't have to accept my assessment of this event because it can be heard on You Tube; "Millichope recital July 2016!" It was a nerve-racking experience, which I'm not sure I will repeat, but it doesn't sound too bad.

I have entitled this chapter 'Music and Friends', although there is no particular reason to lump them together, but, as friends have been so important to me throughout my life, they warrant some coverage. One close friend is, indeed, a musician; Christopher Haines is a good clarinetist and he and I have played (he would say, massacred) many quite ambitious pieces over the years. Whenever we meet, we head for the piano, the clarinet comes out and away we go. We even gave a recital where we were joined by a parrot who squawked insistently throughout the slow movement; we had to stop when our small audience, having sniggered for several minutes, finally dissolved in hysterics! He and his wife, Christine, have been ideal holiday companions over many years.

I still have several close friends from Cambridge, and so far only one of them, poor Leon Brittan, has died. By and large they live scattered around the country and we meet up two or three times a year. We have all remained very close; there is something special about friends made in the late teens and early 20s. These are formative years, when you are in the process of discovering what life is all about. Memories, often of competitive pursuit of the few pretty girls at Cambridge, still come readily to mind. The Wakefield brothers, Robert Skepper, Simon Cairns, David Cobbold, John Mansfield and Oliver Rena, with Freddie Delouche and Bill Spiegelberg, all come into this category. I first knew them as bachelors and, since university, they have all married, remained married to the same woman and I am in love with all their wives: Catherine, Victoria, cousin Hannah, Amanda, Christine, Fiona, Sally, Diana and Rosie!

Very important also has been Annette, Sarah's best friend from Trinity College, Dublin. Sarah and I have had many happy holidays with her and Juan exploring the wonders of Spain; tours of Andalucia, Extremadura, Galicia, Zaragoza, and many other areas spring to mind, and in many cases we stayed at the wonderful Parador Hotels. Bernadette Rendall, who married my cousin Tom, is another very special lady; she is the daughter of a French naval officer and became the queen of Chanel in London.

We attended a dinner at the French Ambassador's house in Kensington, to honour her contribution to French business in London.

Not much of my youth was spent in Shropshire, and it was only in my 30s and 40s that I began to make friends there. Tennis and shooting have brought me together with some lasting friends, particularly David and Ruth Scott, Roger and Annie Gabb, and Hugh and Fayne Meynell. David, Roger, Hugh and I have played tennis together for over 30 years, with Johnny Stevens and Rob Bland. Even now, although increasingly geriatric, we still play most Mondays, although a persistent shoulder problem has latterly reduced me to the indignity of serving underarm. Hugh is now 85 and still plays very well.

In the 50s and 60s, I remember social life in Shropshire being pretty uninspiring: farming, horses and shooting were the main topics of conversation, which I found of limited interest at that stage of my life. However, while that was true of the west of the county, in the east, between Bridgnorth and Wolverhampton, business people from Wolverhampton made most of the running and I found them more fun. I had known a few of the older generation when our shoot at Millichope was let to a syndicate from Wolverhampton, led by Malcolm Graham, the owner of the Midland News group, including *The Express and Star, The Shropshire Star* and *The Shropshire Magazine.* He was a larger-than-life figure whom I admired and respected very much. We used to have shoot lunches followed by teas, at the Crown Hotel in Munslow. Malcolm and the rest of the guns used to descend the steps from the pub to their cars after tea, having probably drunk half bottle of whisky each, during the course of the day. They would then drive their Rolls Royces and Bentleys home. Malcolm lived to his late eighties, having smoked two packs of du Maurier cigarettes every day. Although a generation older, he was a good friend over many years, and I am pleased to say that Sarah and I used to go on playing bridge with Malcolm and his third wife, Barbara, until nearly the end.

Many of these families from the east of the county used to play poker in the evenings and as a bachelor, I was a popular dinner guest because I nearly always lost; playing five and seven card stud would usually cost me about £50-£60. It didn't stop me going, however, because these evenings were good fun.

In the early 80s, Sarah and I met Christopher and Jenny Bland at a dinner party in Hampshire. Sarah was seated next to Christopher and discovered that he was looking for a spaniel puppy, and it just so happened that she had some for sale. The next week, Christopher and Jenny drove up to Shropshire, and they bought Sam, a black-and-white ten-week old puppy who grew into a very special dog. When he died, a dozen years later they were inconsolable. That transaction was a good start and we began to see a good deal of them. Christopher, at that stage, was a keen shot and became a regular visitor to Millichope. They lived at Abbots Worthy on the edge of Winchester, and we went down for many enjoyable weekends. They also acquired a *manoir* in the Gers in France, in a village called Jegun, between Auch and Condom, with a swimming pool, a tennis court and a vineyard which, although fruitful, did not produce a good wine. Christopher equipped his vineyard with all the latest kit, but he served such illustrious bottles at the main meal times that the home-grown product only got a look in at elevenses in the morning!

These parties were full of entertaining guests, many from the media who, over the years, we got to know well. Simon Jenkins, in particular, has remained close and we regularly go and see him at his special converted village hall, on the seafront at Aberdovey. Max and Penny Hastings were regular guests, too. I once played a gruellingly competitive singles tennis game with Penny on the court at Abbots Worthy, before breakfast. The court was in a scruffy condition, covered in leaves, and it was a tough, competitive match. When we returned to the breakfast table after two hard-fought sets, Max looked up from the novel he was reading and cocked an eyebrow at Penny. 'Well,' he asked. 'Did you win?'

I followed Christopher's career with some awe. After several successful early ventures, he made some serious money out of London Weekend Television, at the time of the award of the franchises, only to lose the company shortly afterwards to a takeover bid by Granada. He then became chairman of the BBC, to be followed by the chairmanship of British Telecom, before becoming chairman of the Royal Shakespeare Company, for whom he raised a fortune, only to end his life as a budding novelist, with two successful novels and a play to his credit. Finally, he succumbed to prostate cancer and died after two fairly wretched years at the age of 78. This happened in the same year that Leon Brittan died, also the victim of a series of cancers.

Music and Friends

Over the years, Leon came to stay with us many times and we spent happy weekends in Yorkshire with him and Diana, his wife, whom we first met on a beach in Saltburn-on-Sea. She was getting divorced at the time and contact between her and Leon had to be somewhat furtive. He had two Yorkshire constituencies, first Whitby and then Richmond. Despite an urban Jewish background, he took to Yorkshire like a duck to water and, in due course, became accepted and, indeed, much liked by the grand county figures who proliferate up there. Diana is a remarkable woman, who became chairman of the National Lottery Community Fund, among numerous other *pro bono publico* appointments. She had two daughters, one of whom, Catherine, married David McGarvey, an academic from Paisley with whom I share a love of music, and he and Catherine have a beautiful daughter, Iona. Leon was an enthusiastic step-father, whom his grandchildren likened to a Tigger!

Following his retirement from the European Commission, Leon had an extended spell working for UBS, the Swiss bank, for whom he travelled incessantly all over the world doing deals. In his mid-seventies, he developed cancer and had a dreadful final year, made worse by utterly disgraceful allegations of sexual misconduct by a hopelessly unreliable witness, slavishly and unforgivably believed by the police. In poor Leon's case, they didn't even bother to inform him that they had dropped the charges against him before he died. Both Christopher and Leon, however, had the most magnificent memorial services, which I shall never forget.

Christopher and Ginny Palmer Tomkinson, in recent

years, have been good friends. They are regular visitors to Jura, where Christopher is one of the fittest people I know on the hill, and we've also had a lot of fun in business together, since he engineered my joining the board of Electric and General. He also helped Frank get his first job at Cazenove. He has been a true friend.

This is by no means a complete list. There are so many others who have played a part in my life, and Sarah and I still keep meeting people who we would like to see a lot more of, but we cannot fit them all in! The pressures of life are such that there is not enough time for so many things we want to do, and so many people with whom we would like to spend more time. It is certainly true that when including 'A Lot of Luck' in the title of this book, I meant above all Sarah and my family, as well as my wonderful friends.

Chapter Twenty-Five
The Future

At this stage of a memoir, the writer usually indulges himself in delivering his views on the state of the world (it is nearly always 'his' views because the overwhelming preponderance of memoirs are written by men!) and this is usually accompanied by a look into the future, normally pretty gloomy.

I'm sorry to say that I have not been able to resist adding to the number of armchair pundits and, as is invariably the case, I feel that my views are possibly worth an airing and beg the reader's indulgence for setting out some of them.

The first thing to say is that I believe my generation has been uniquely privileged in living in the second half of the 20th century. The world has seen an unprecedented surge in prosperity, with a huge increase in standards of living in most of the advanced countries. When I look back on Britain in the 1950s (not to mention Berlin!), and compare living standards then with the way we live now, the advances have been astonishing. Democratic governments have, on the whole, served us well and we have been able to say and do almost anything we like, with a huge increase in affordable travel and a bewildering profusion of options in life. We have inherited a standard of living that has been made possible by the cumulative hard work and ingenuity of previous generations, achieved often amid conditions of grinding poverty. We don't have to work like that now; automated machines and computers have taken over most

The Future

physical work and routine office chores. Modern medicine has enabled us to extend our lifespan by about 10 years, since the war. To judge from the media, however, all this doesn't seem to have made us happier, but then, newspapers exist to make money and bad stories sell better than cheerful ones.

At present, there are signs that the good times may be coming to an end, as good times always do. Parliamentary democracy is coming under pressure from populist parties in Europe, and new forms of communication enabled by the Internet which, adopted by billions of consumers all round the world, have the potential to cause a lot of harm. This potential is already being realised; it would have been unthinkable for a man like Trump to become president of the United States even 20 years ago. In Britain, the vote for Brexit in the referendum was largely the result of dissatisfaction with the government, as a result of the ten years of austerity which followed the 2007/8 financial crash. It was easy to focus this discontent on immigrants and a vague nostalgia for the old days, encapsulated by the slogan, 'Let's take back control.' I found this unpersuasive and voted to remain in the EU. The next 50 years, I feel, will bring us a bumpier ride than the late 20th century.

I wish to concentrate these comments, however, on business and the environment, the two arenas of life which have absorbed most of my time and energy over the last fifty years.

Starting with business, it is my conviction that most British people are generally not interested in business or, indeed, in their jobs; when working in middle management, as many do, they would much rather be doing something else. Making money is somehow disreputable, and those who succeed at it are usually suspected of cutting corners or doing something underhand. In novels and fiction generally, big business and 'multinational corporations' in particular, are normally cast as villains. We are also quite an envious lot, and other peoples' success is often hard to bear! It is certainly high time for entrepreneurs building up companies and, indeed, perhaps even speculators, to stage a rally in public esteem. It should be better recognised that speculators play an important role in mitigating extreme swings in prices, whether of commodities, currencies, or anything else. Collectively they perform a service. I am impressed that my old friend and boss, Michael Stoddart, describes himself on his passport as 'Speculator'.

The British certainly haven't been good at running big businesses. Take the car industry: after the war we had many of Europe's dominant marques – Austin, Morris, Rover, Jaguar, Hillman, MG, Rolls-Royce and Bentley, to name but some. They have all now been taken over by foreign owners or have closed. Volkswagen, which hardly existed after the war, is with Toyota, now the largest car company in the world. Our press used to comment on this with resentment and envy. Could it be, though, that the Germans and, indeed, the Japanese are simply a more disciplined and industrious people than the British, more tolerant of discipline, with more committed, focused and energetic management? The same story can be repeated over most of our leading industries, which have succumbed to foreign competition. Few of the companies controlling the commanding heights of the UK economy are still British. We are reasonably good at retailing and we are certainly good at establishing markets and financial wheeling and dealing, as in the City of London. But it is disappointing to many observers that a large and increasing number of British workers, including most of those in the City, now work for foreigners. Brexit is not going to change this.

Most of my experience comes from working with small and medium-sized companies, during my years working in the Midlands. Here there were numerous family businesses which were, in many cases, strong, robust companies in the post-war years, but all too often, the sons of the founding fathers neglected their inheritance and preferred a life of country pursuits, fishing and shooting. In the Wolverhampton area, there were many such companies, where the elder son and heir neglected the business, with predictable results. There are exceptions, of course, and recently we have seen a few stellar examples of British success; JCB, Dyson and ARM come to mind. I do, however, doubt the assertion by those who favour Brexit, that once British business is released from the dead hand of Brussels bureaucracy, regulations and form filling, our businesses will leap ahead like branches of a cedar tree freed of a covering of snow. I can see little evidence that this is likely to happen.

I am not among those who foresee disaster, with rising unemployment and a collapse in living standards. I think that after a period of five or ten years, Britain will be much the same as it is now; shambling along, gently losing its place in the world, with few people caring very much.

Coming to specific issues, we are told that it is a criminal shame that our best companies often sell out to foreign acquirers, when they should be building and investing to become world-class companies. In an ideal world, this would be so, but being more realistic, in the UK we are much better at building up small companies than we are at running big ones. I think the founding families of private companies, who often never saw any real cash during the years they were building up their businesses, are well advised to take the money, providing they see a price that adequately reflects their achievement and, hopefully, the next generation will start a new dynamic company (so long as the sons don't spend their father's cash on slow horses and fast women).

I also think that being quoted on the stock exchange is not always helpful. I, of all people, have no reason to complain about the fate of the various companies, upon whose boards I served. Certainly, for a fast-growing technology company requiring capital for expansion, a high price-earnings ratio can be invaluable in raising capital cheaply. This probably also applies to pharmaceutical companies whose activities are more conceptual, with the rewards likely to appear over a longer period.

However, there is another side to the coin; being quoted is expensive, with onerous reporting requirements, and there is also only a very limited period when directors are free to deal in their own shares. Even then the market is only happy when directors are buying; selling is never welcome.

More importantly, I also think the treatment of acquisition accounting has been very suspect, until recent reforms. For example, during my active business life there were many conglomerate companies whose growth was fuelled by acquisitions, made possible by a high share price. Companies such as BTR and Hanson Trust for example, bought a great many companies. After the takeover, the first priority was to improve the profitability of the acquired company. This involved writing down the stock and work in progress, making provisions for everything in sight, and then putting up the prices of the company's products. This could sharply improve the short-term profits and make the acquisition look like a good deal, resulting in a better share price and thereby enabling further acquisitions. The trouble was that the target company's basic business was weakened and price increases would lead to loss of market share. In short, the all-important goal of the high share price was achieved at the expense of the target company's competitive position. This was certainly not in the interests of UK plc.

The stock exchange is often accused of bringing an increase in short-termism; investors, understandably, like reasonably quick returns by way of the payment of dividends or, even better, sharp increases in the share price. There are two sides to this coin. Keynes said, 'In the long run, we are all dead', and it is true that many inept managements blame shareholders for being impatient and greedy with excessively short time horizons. Nonetheless, patience is generally a virtue in investing, and short-termism can be a real problem; the activities of hedge funds, arbitrageurs and computerised traders, can result in sound, well-run businesses becoming vulnerable to bids by financial operators, impatient for quick results. Personally, I am sad to see the demise of GKN which during my career has been by far the best of our larger engineering companies.

Corporate governance is another area of business that has gone mad. I remember a board meeting at Sage, where we spent three and a half hours in the audit committee dotting i's and crossing t's. Then after lunch, we only had two hours to discuss the business in the main board meeting before it was time for the non-executive directors to climb onto planes to fly home. After the departure of Michael Jackson, our next chairman was Tony Hobson, chairman of the audit committee at Sage. He had previously been chairman of the audit committee at HBOS, which effectively went bankrupt, after neglecting all the fundamental principles of sound banking, and had to be bailed out by Lloyds Bank. I wonder if the risks of borrowing short and lending long are to be found on a bank's 'risk register'? Probably not.

Sound corporate governance is, of course, essential in any properly run company, but too much of it is a case of 'motherhood and apple pie', and a massive waste of directors' time.

Finally, I do think that greed and lack of principle generally is too prevalent in business, as in much of public life in the UK. At least chairmen of commercial companies

The Future

can be held to account quite quickly for the statements they make. If they get it wrong, they get sacked or sometimes go to jail. This is not the case in politics: the scale of the lies told by politicians in the weeks of the referendum was breathtaking but, unlike businessmen, politicians usually get away with it. Greed was possibly every bit as bad in the early post-war years, but I don't remember anything on the scale of the recent sale by Philip Green of British Home Stores, who, having taken out £1 billion in dividend, sold the company for a nominal sum. This deal, in the absence of government intervention, would have resulted in a loss to the BHS pensioners of over £500 million. I do believe that on the whole people behaved better fifty years ago; 'My word is my bond' really used to mean something.

On a more cheerful note, I should also say that a career in business can be immensely rewarding in more ways than just the making of money. The excitement of having judged an opportunity right, and seeing a surge in the value of a company's shares is something that still sends my pulse racing. From Lesney Products back in the '60s, right through to various investments made in my retirement, I have loved looking for winners on the stock market. I have also enjoyed some wonderful partnerships in my career with Roger Foster, David Backhouse, Micky Ingall and John Harris among others. It has been a privilege working with such people and I have certainly enjoyed almost every phase of my own career.

After the main years of my active business career, during my fifties and sixties when I was mostly a non-executive director, I began to spend an increasing amount of time on environmental issues. I became a green! This caused a certain amount of bewilderment and impatience among my friends. Surely there are more important things to worry about than bugs and bees and even the survival of an obscure snake in the West Indies (the subject of one of Fauna and Flora's programmes). At dinner parties, my neighbour's eyes, usually female, would glaze over when the subject came up. It is bad form to be serious about anything at dinner parties and nobody likes hearing about long-term threats. On a national level, environmental charities have been right down at the bottom of favoured outlets for donations. Until recently, under 1% was the proportion of charitable spending allocated to green causes. Unlike Germany, greens are largely unrepresented in the British parliament. Spreading the word has been tough going.

My early interest originated in all the wildlife holidays which Sarah and I used to take, leading to my becoming a director of a number of green charities, notably FFI. I really minded about the prospect of extinctions. Some extinctions are inevitable, and they happen all the time, but to live with so many mammals, birds, reptiles, and even insects, facing extinction within my lifetime filled me with incomprehension and, indeed, anger. How could people be so indifferent to the fate of the creatures that share the planet with us?

It would be nice to report that the pace of destruction has relented somewhat, and that some species are making a rally. If anything, the reverse is happening and the pace of destruction is accelerating. There is no let-up in deforestation

The Future

worldwide, while over the last 10 years the decimation of the major mammals through the poaching of elephants, rhinoceros and other species has been fuelled by sky-high prices being paid for ivory and rhino horn, driven by Far Eastern demand for their supposed (and utterly bogus) erotic enhancement properties. Tigers are possibly doing a bit better, if we can trust the figures coming from the Indian Government, but this can't last much longer with the pressure of human population enveloping the last remaining minute forest reserves. Why should I worry about the fate of these creatures? Well, I just do. Can anything be done about it? Probably not much, but I am encouraged by signs of a belated change in public attitudes.

One factor in this has been the emergence of climate change as a world problem. Fortunately, it affects human beings; we see pictures on television of commuters scurrying around in Beijing and Delhi wearing smog masks, reminiscent of those worn in London in the early 1950s. I inwardly rejoice and say thank God for that! There are still a few doubters, our ex-Chancellor Nigel Lawson prominent among them, but they have lost the battle and the world's governments are set on doing something to relieve the causes of man-made environmental pollution. Even Trump's move to pull America out of the Paris climate change agreement will make very little difference; most major world corporations, even including previously spectacular disbelievers such as Exxon, are now converts. There is currently a growing belief among governments that something has to be done to stem the devastating increase in plastic in the world's oceans. The two astonishing Blue Planet films from the BBC have, I am sure, been responsible for the oceans beginning to feature on the political agenda. The world is slowly beginning to take notice. The concept of natural capital is also gaining attention; we have been consuming the earth's natural capital, trees, water, soil, minerals, animals, birds, and it is partly this that has made possible the phenomenal increase in living standards since the war. But this is not sustainable. If India, China, Indonesia and other third world countries were to achieve a comparable standard of living to the West (which is exactly what they aspire to), we would need to exploit the resources of several additional planets.

It is quite possible that it is now too late to do anything about the rise in CO_2 levels. This is not only increasing, but the rate of increase is accelerating. The world is going to have to come up with some radical solutions, and we have very little time in which to do it.

On a personal level, I am planning to plant a 130-acre woodland on a steep escarpment on Jura. This is on a bleak site swept by gales on poor land but, before being written off as a lunatic, I would say that I have now been planting trees on Jura for thirty years and have built up a bit of experience on where they're likely to prosper. It will incorporate a range of native hardwoods, together with Scots pine. Imagine my delight to be offered the chance of applying for a carbon credit! This could bring in £80,000, and is a practical example of how, by effectively selling the air above my wood, I can enable a polluting company to buy an offsetting credit. There are a number of agents now

The Future

dealing specifically in carbon credits. This is something which our Global Canopy Programme, has been working to popularize, and at last it is really happening. If countries in the tropics could plant several billion trees a year, where they really grow fast, this could before too long make a real impact on CO_2 levels, while improving biodiversity, water supply and air quality.

Is that likely to happen anytime soon? Sadly, no.

Scallop dredging in the Inner Hebrides of Scotland is a local problem in which I have taken an interest. This involves scallop fishermen, instead of diving for scallops, dragging heavy dredges along the seabed, trashing the marine environment with very bad effects on spawning grounds for fish, as well as creel fishing for crabs and lobsters. They do it right outside our window in Jura, where the sea bed has been reduced in areas to a submarine desert. We don't catch lobsters and crabs any more in our pots! Bird watching, diving and marine tourism have already suffered. The dredgers are well organised, and are powerful lobbyists with Marine Scotland, who decide on the whereabouts and number of Marine Protection Areas. I have been trying to influence the people of Jura to take a stand against dredging; so far with little success. The view was that a cessation could imperil jobs somewhere. However, I switched tack and commissioned a submarine film to be made by Mark Woombs, a marine biologist and diver, who took some spectacular pictures of a beautiful sea loch called Sunart, about eighty miles north of Jura. After seeing this, I commissioned him to do a similar film on Loch Tarbert, the sea loch that nearly bisects the island.

A Shaky Start and a Lot of Luck

This was a great success. He made a magnificent series of slides and we invited the whole island to come and watch (with the added inducement of wine and cheese). The turnout was tremendous, and most of the adults on the whole island came along. He preceded our presentation with a show for the schoolchildren and accompanied the film with graphic descriptions of what these various marine creatures were and what they were doing. Even at thirty meters underwater, it was all sex and violence! The colours in parts of the loch were nearly as good as those of the barrier reef in the tropics. As luck would have it, my film was closely followed by Blue Planet 2 from the BBC, which showed some of the most astonishing footage ever taken underwater. I think this will increase awareness of these problems on Jura. Increasing awareness and education is absolutely the way to go, and the viewing figures of wildlife programmes suggest that the public is responding. Meanwhile, the dredging battle continues!

Over the last ten years, we have seen the mass migration of refugees into Europe from the Middle East and North Africa, even down as far as Nigeria. Initially, the majority of them were refugees from civil strife in Syria, Afghanistan and other theatres of conflict. Increasingly, now they are coming from countries such as Eritrea, Somalia, Egypt, Ethiopia and Nigeria. These refugees in many cases are fleeing from hunger, mainly caused by environmental degradation and overpopulation. Looking further ahead, say 50-100 years, a new factor may well come into play, namely a substantial rise in sea levels as a consequence of global warming. Depending on the extent of the rise of

The Future

CO_2 levels, the rise could be several feet. This would imperil many of the world's great coastal cities. Given time, the more affluent of these would probably be able to establish some defences. However, in poor countries the consequence will probably be mass migrations. Europe (or Europe plus the UK!) will continue to be a magnet and immigration will become the overwhelming issue. We have already had a foretaste of this in the last two or three years. It is safe to bet that it will become much worse. All these problems may seem remote, 50-100 years is a long time, but it is within the probable lifespan of our own grandchildren and, certainly, great grandchildren. What kind of legacy are we leaving them?

There are a few encouraging signs; population growth, at least in the Far East and the developed countries, has moderated (although life expectancy is increasing). In Africa and other areas of the world, however, growth rates remain very high. Encouraging figures are now emerging, suggesting that world demand for most commodities has already peaked, which could release large areas of land and thus enable some re-wilding to take place, with an increase in biodiversity. I very much hope this happens.

It is not beyond the wit of humankind to resolve these problems, but I would have thought it will require an unprecedented level of international cooperation, and whether democracy is capable of managing it, I rather doubt. Many people tell me that they vote for such and such an issue (Brexit being one), saying they are doing it for their grandchildren. I would have thought environmental problems will be much more of a worry for their grandchildren and should now be the most pressing concern of all governments on the planet.

There is always hope. Humans are resourceful and clever, and if we can work together on an international level, with sufficient resources and commitment, these problems might be solved. Unfortunately, this is not going to happen in my lifetime; things need to get much worse before a consensus will arise to make them better.

Epilogue

To finish on a personal note, seventy-three years ago my father, in that memorable letter to me before setting off for Normandy on his final journey, wrote,

> *'I fear there has not been enough money to keep on the lovely home we once had at Millichope However, let us hope you are still in the neighbourhood and the estate has not had to be sold.'*

As it turns out, Sarah and I have been able to keep the show on the road for another generation. I do take immense pleasure that Millichope Park, the house, now looks more beautiful than ever and Frank and Tonie are full of exciting plans for the house and for the estate. Harriet has now moved into her charming house in Corfton, two villages up the road from Munslow, the grandchildren are growing up in settled and happy homes, and we are lucky enough to see a lot of them; for busy parents, grannies and grandpas can be quite useful! Baby-sitting, viewing school plays, watching cricket matches and attending first communions, collecting them from school and taking them back again, are all very agreeable jobs that fall to grandparents, and Sarah and I have loved this phase of our lives. Sarah was the prime mover in our move to Tugford, where we have now lived for the last seven years, and she master-minded the renovation of the house. It is a pleasure to live there in the middle of the hamlet of Tugford, surrounded by the beautiful garden that she has made.

Epilogue

Growing up in the immediate post-war years was quite different. The present world in many ways bears little resemblance to that of my childhood and youth. Nevertheless some essential pillars remain; moral standards seem to remain largely unchanged, religion still clings on, although the devout belief that was so central to my mother's life seems rare nowadays.

I certainly hope that my grandchildren will find a way of adapting and prospering in this confusing world which we now inhabit, and that they will be prepared for the squalls that inevitably lie ahead.

Meanwhile, we have much for which to be thankful.

Tugford, May 2018